Getting Started with Raspberry Pi Zero

Get started with the smallest, cheapest, and
highest-utility Pi ever—Raspberry Pi Zero

Richard Grimmett

PUBLISHING

BIRMINGHAM - MUMBAI

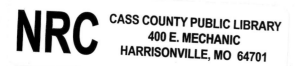

Getting Started with Raspberry Pi Zero

First published: March 2016

Production reference: 1210316

Published by Packt Publishing Ltd.
Livery Place
35 Livery Street
Birmingham B3 2PB, UK.

ISBN 978-1-78646-946-5

www.packtpub.com

Credits

Author
Richard Grimmett

Reviewer
David Whale

Commissioning Editor
Kartikey Pandey

Acquisition Editor
Tushar Gupta

Content Development Editor
Merint Thomas Mathew

Technical Editor
Saurabh Malhotra

Copy Editors
Kevin McGowan
Sneha Singh

Project Coordinator
Francina Pinto

Proofreader
Safis Editing

Indexer
Priya Sane

Graphics
Disha Haria

Production Coordinator
Shantanu N. Zagade

Cover Work
Shantanu N. Zagade

About the Author

Richard Grimmett has always been fascinated by computers and electronics since his very first programming project that used Fortran on punch cards. He has a bachelor's and master's degree in electrical engineering and a PhD in leadership studies. He also has 26 years of experience in the radar and telecommunications industries, and even has one of the original brick phones. He now teaches computer science and electrical engineering at the Brigham Young University, Idaho, where his office is filled with his numerous robotics projects.

This book is the result of working with the wonderful students at BYU-Idaho. It also wouldn't be possible without the help of my wonderful wife, Jeanne.

About the Reviewer

David Whale is a software developer living in Essex, UK. He started coding as a schoolboy aged 11, inspired by the school science technician to build his own computer from a kit and quickly progressed to writing machine code programs because they were "small and fast". These early experiments led to some of his code being used inside a saleable educational word game when he was only 13.

He has been developing software professionally ever since, mainly writing small and fast code that goes into electronic products, including automated machinery, electric cars, mobile phones, energy meters, and wireless doorbells.

These days, he runs his own software consultancy called Thinking Binaries and spends nearly half of his time helping to design the next wave of the Internet called The Internet of Things, by connecting electronic devices to it. The rest of the time he volunteers for The Institution of Engineering and Technology, running training courses for teachers, designing and running workshops and clubs for school children, and being busy with his Raspberry Pi, BBC micro:bit and Arduino.

He was the technical editor for the book *Adventures in Raspberry Pi* and the co-author of the book *Adventures in Minecraft*, and is a regular reviewer and editor of technical books from a number of book publishers.

I was really pleased to be asked to review this great new book of projects using the Raspberry Pi Zero. The size of the Pi Zero makes it ideal for building into other products. In this book, Richard Grimmett takes us on an amazing journey of circuit bending, coding, and innovating using this tiny computer! But don't stop here; the projects in this book will give you the skills you need and inspire you to come up with many new ideas yourself!

www.PacktPub.com

eBooks, discount offers, and more

Did you know that Packt offers eBook versions of every book published, with PDF and ePub files available? You can upgrade to the eBook version at www.PacktPub. com and as a print book customer, you are entitled to a discount on the eBook copy. Get in touch with us at customercare@packtpub.com for more details.

At www.PacktPub.com, you can also read a collection of free technical articles, sign up for a range of free newsletters and receive exclusive discounts and offers on Packt books and eBooks.

https://www2.packtpub.com/books/subscription/packtlib

Do you need instant solutions to your IT questions? PacktLib is Packt's online digital book library. Here, you can search, access, and read Packt's entire library of books.

Why subscribe?

- Fully searchable across every book published by Packt
- Copy and paste, print, and bookmark content
- On demand and accessible via a web browser

Table of Contents

Preface

For many years, robots and other advanced electronic wonders could only be seen on the television, movies, or in university or military labs. In recent years, however, the availability of new and inexpensive hardware and also free and open source software, has provided the opportunity for almost anyone with a little technical knowledge and imagination to build these technical wonders. The first wave of projects were fueled by Arduino, an inexpensive and simple-to-program microcontroller. The next wave was carried further by the introduction of the Raspberry Pi, an even more capable processor powered by the Linux operating system.

Now there is an even less expensive, powerful microprocessor: the Raspberry Pi Zero. This little processor packs a processor powerful enough to run Linux into a small and even less expensive package. This capability, coupled with some additional power, inexpensive hardware, and free open source software provides a platform for projects that range from simple wheeled robots to advanced flying machines.

What this book covers

Chapter 1, Setting Started with Raspberry Pi Zero, is designed to go through the details of setting up a useful development environment on Raspberry Pi Zero. The chapter begins with a discussion of how to connect power and continues through setting up a full system, configured and ready to be connected to any of the amazing devices and SW capabilities to develop advanced robotics applications.

Chapter 2, Programming Raspberry Pi Zero, reviews, for those who are already familiar, basic Linux, editing, and programming techniques that will be useful through the rest of the book. You'll learn how to interact from the command line, how to create and edit a file using an editor, and basic Python programming.

Chapter 3, *Accessing the GPIO Pins on Raspberry Pi Zero*, discusses the GPIO capabilities of Raspberry Pi Zero by building and controlling some simple LED circuits.

Chapter 4, *Building and Controlling a Simple Wheeled Robot*, discusses one of the amazing things you can do with Raspberry Pi Zero, controlling a simple wheeled robot. This chapter will show you how to add motor control, so you can build your very own autonomous mobile robot.

Chapter 5, *Building a Robot That Can Walk*, tells us about another impressive robotic project, an autonomous robot that can walk. This is done using servos whose position can be controlled using Raspberry Pi and some additional USB-controlled hardware.

Chapter 6, *Adding Voice Recognition and Speech – A Voice Activated Robot*, tells us about a voice-activated robot. One of the significant new features of today's computer system is the ability to input commands and provide output without a screen or keyboard. A few years ago, the concept of a computer that can talk and listen was science fiction, but today it is becoming a standard part of new cell phones. This chapter introduces how Raspberry Pi Zero can both listen to speech and also respond in kind. This is not as easy as it sounds (pun intended) and you'll be exposed to some basic functionality, while also understanding some of the key limitations. You'll take a standard toy and turn it into a responsive robot.

Chapter 7, *Adding Raspberry Pi Zero to an RC Vehicle*, tells us about another astounding capability of Raspberry Pi Zero, the ability to add "sight" to you projects. Raspberry Pi Zero makes this very easy by supporting open source software and readily available USB webcams. By adding this and a remote control, you can build a remote control vehicle that can go around corners, into rooms, wherever you'd like to go.

Chapter 8, *Playing Rock, Paper, or Scissors with Raspberry Pi Zero*, tells us about how we can use our toolkit to build and control a robotic hand that can see and respond to the world around it. In this case, you'll program your hand to play rock, paper, and scissors.

Chapter 9, *Adding Raspberry Pi Zero to a Quadcopter*, talks about the fact that building a robot that can walk, talk, or play air hockey is cool, but one that can fly is the ultimate goal.

What you need for this book

You need a Raspberry Pi Zero. You can refer to the software list along with the code bundle of the book.

Who this book is for

This book is designed for the beginner. It requires little more than a vivid imagination and a desire to learn the basics of programming and hardware configuration.

Conventions

In this book, you will find a number of text styles that distinguish between different kinds of information. Here are some examples of these styles and an explanation of their meaning.

Code words in text, database table names, folder names, filenames, file extensions, pathnames, dummy URLs, user input, and Twitter handles are shown as follows: "To install Nmap, type `sudo apt-get install nmap`. To run Nmap, type `sudo nmap -sp 10.25.155.1/154`."

A block of code is set as follows:

```
a = input("Input value: ")
b = input("Input second value: ")
c = a + b
print c
```

When we wish to draw your attention to a particular part of a code block, the relevant lines or items are set in bold:

```
a = input("Input value: ")
b = input("Input second value: ")
c = a + b
print c
```

Any command-line input or output is written as follows:

```
cd /home/pi/Desktop
```

New terms and **important words** are shown in bold. Words that you see on the screen, for example, in menus or dialog boxes, appear in the text like this: "Clicking on the **Scan** selector scans for all the devices connected to the network."

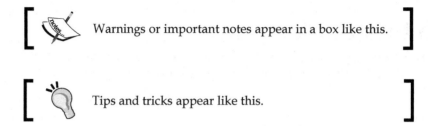

Warnings or important notes appear in a box like this.

Tips and tricks appear like this.

Reader feedback

Feedback from our readers is always welcome. Let us know what you think about this book — what you liked or disliked. Reader feedback is important for us as it helps us develop titles that you will really get the most out of.

To send us general feedback, simply e-mail feedback@packtpub.com, and mention the book's title in the subject of your message.

If there is a topic that you have expertise in and you are interested in either writing or contributing to a book, see our author guide at www.packtpub.com/authors.

Customer support

Now that you are the proud owner of a Packt book, we have a number of things to help you to get the most from your purchase.

Downloading the example code

You can download the example code files for this book from your account at http://www.packtpub.com. If you purchased this book elsewhere, you can visit http://www.packtpub.com/support and register to have the files e-mailed directly to you.

You can download the code files by following these steps:

1. Log in or register to our website using your e-mail address and password.
2. Hover the mouse pointer on the **SUPPORT** tab at the top.

3. Click on **Code Downloads & Errata**.

4. Enter the name of the book in the **Search** box.

5. Select the book for which you're looking to download the code files.

6. Choose from the drop-down menu where you purchased this book from.

7. Click on **Code Download**.

Once the file is downloaded, please make sure that you unzip or extract the folder using the latest version of:

- WinRAR/7-Zip for Windows

- Zipeg/iZip/UnRarX for Mac

- 7-Zip/PeaZip for Linux

Downloading the color images of this book

We also provide you with a PDF file that has color images of the screenshots/ diagrams used in this book. The color images will help you better understand the changes in the output. You can download this file from `http://www.packtpub.com/sites/default/files/downloads/GettingStartedwithRaspberryPiZero_ColorImages.pdf`.

Errata

Although we have taken every care to ensure the accuracy of our content, mistakes do happen. If you find a mistake in one of our books—maybe a mistake in the text or the code—we would be grateful if you could report this to us. By doing so, you can save other readers from frustration and help us improve subsequent versions of this book. If you find any errata, please report them by visiting `http://www.packtpub.com/submit-errata`, selecting your book, clicking on the **Errata Submission Form** link, and entering the details of your errata. Once your errata are verified, your submission will be accepted and the errata will be uploaded to our website or added to any list of existing errata under the Errata section of that title.

To view the previously submitted errata, go to `https://www.packtpub.com/books/content/support` and enter the name of the book in the search field. The required information will appear under the **Errata** section.

Piracy

Piracy of copyrighted material on the Internet is an ongoing problem across all media. At Packt, we take the protection of our copyright and licenses very seriously. If you come across any illegal copies of our works in any form on the Internet, please provide us with the location address or website name immediately so that we can pursue a remedy.

Please contact us at copyright@packtpub.com with a link to the suspected pirated material.

We appreciate your help in protecting our authors and our ability to bring you valuable content.

Questions

If you have a problem with any aspect of this book, you can contact us at questions@packtpub.com, and we will do our best to address the problem.

1
Getting Started with Raspberry Pi Zero

There has been a major shift in electronics and computer accessibility driven by the introduction of the Raspberry Pi microcomputer and its variants. With a completely different price point along with a significantly expanded support community, the Raspberry Pi has been an unprecedented success in bringing inexpensive computing to a wide audience. The Raspberry Pi Zero continues with that important approach, providing unprecedented computer power at an even lower price point.

The Raspberry Pi Zero is particularly useful as it can be paired with inexpensive hardware and open-source software to do a wide range of different Do-It-Yourself projects. You'll learn about many of these in this book. You'll learn how to control DC motors, how to control servos, how to hook up a microphone for speech recognition, and even how to connect a webcam to view and interpret the outside world.

The Raspberry Pi Zero can do amazing things, but first you'll need to understand how to access all of this capability. In this chapter, you'll learn how to:

- Provide power to the board
- Connect a display, keyboard, and mouse
- Load and configure the operating system
- Configure the board for remote access

Setting up the Raspberry Pi Zero

While the Raspberry Pi Zero is a powerful computer, you'll need some additional hardware to access this capability. Here are the items that you'll need for this chapter's projects:

- A Raspberry Pi Zero
- A micro USB cable and power supply to provide power to the board
- A display with an HDMI video input
- A keyboard, a mouse, and a powered USB hub
- A microSD card – with at least 4 GB capacity
- A microSD card writer
- Another computer that is connected to the Internet
- A WLAN USB dongle
- A 40x2 pin connector strip

Before you get started, let's get familiar with the Raspberry Pi Zero. Here is an image of the hardware:

Note that the GPIO pin male headers are not pre-soldered to the board; you'll want to do that. You can buy these at most online electronics retailers. You should also become familiar with the various connections on the board. Here, you can see the Raspberry Pi Zero with the connector soldered and the connections labeled for your information:

Powering the board

One of the first issues you'll want to consider is how to power the board. To do this, you need to connect through the USB power connection. There are two choices to provide power to the Raspberry Pi Zero:

1. Connect the microUSB connector labeled power to a 5V DC source powered by a USB power supply. This can be either a power supply that can plug directly into an outlet or power supplied by a powered USB port like those available on most computers.

2. Connect the microUSB connector to a battery. The simplest connection is to batteries that have a USB connector, like those used to charge cellphones. Here is a image of just such a battery:

In both cases, make sure that the unit can supply enough current. You'll need a supply that can provide at least 1000 mA at 5 volts. There are two USB charge connections on this battery which makes it easy to plug the Raspberry Pi Zero into one and the powered USB hub into the other. Do not plug in the board just yet, you first need to connect the rest of the hardware and configure the microSD card. However, you are now ready to connect the rest of the hardware.

Hooking up a keyboard, mouse, and display

The next step is to connect a keyboard, mouse, and display to the Raspberry Pi Zero. You may have much of this stuff already but, if you don't, there are some things to consider before buying additional equipment. Let's start with the keyboard and mouse.

To connect any device to the Raspberry Pi Zero you'll need some sort of adapter or hub. You can buy a simple hub that goes from the microUSB connector on the Raspberry Pi Zero to the more common standard connector. You can find these at most electronics online retailers, and it looks something like this:

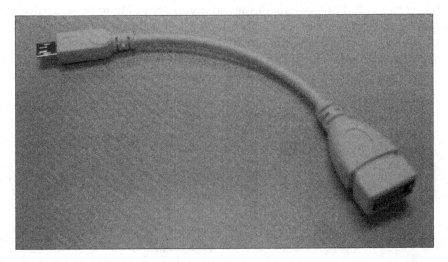

However, there will be projects when you will want to connect more than one device to the Raspberry Pi Zero. For these cases you may want to consider purchasing a powered USB hub. Before deciding on the hub to connect to your board, you need to understand the difference between a powered USB hub and one that gets its power from the USB port itself.

Almost all USB hubs are not powered, in other words, you don't plug in the USB hub separately. The reason for this is that almost all of these hubs are hooked up to computers with very large power supplies and powering USB devices from the computer is not a problem. This is not the case for your board. The USB port on your board has very limited power capabilities so if you are going to hook up devices that require significant power – a WAN adapter or a webcam for instance – you're going to need a powered USB hub, one that provides power to the devices through a separate power source. Here is an image of such a device, available at http://www.amazon.com/ and other online retailers:

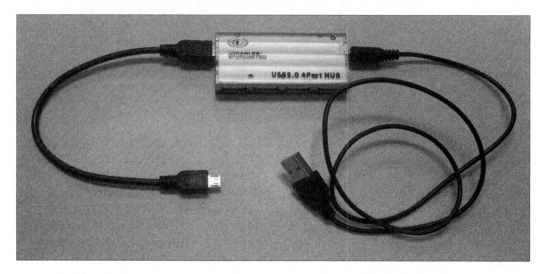

Note that there are two connections on this hub. The one to the far right is a power connection and it will be plugged into a battery or a USB power adapter with a USB port. The connection to the left is the USB connection, which will be plugged into the Raspberry Pi. To connect the power USB board to the Raspberry Pi Zero you need a cable that connects to a microUSB connector. Now, you'll have more connections to add a mouse and keyboard, webcams, and a USB WLAN device.

Now, you'll also need a display. Fortunately, your Raspberry Pi Zero offers lots of choices. There are a number of different video standards; here is an image of some of the most common ones for reference:

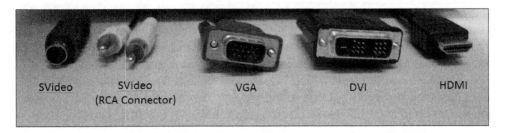

| SVideo | SVideo (RCA Connector) | VGA | DVI | HDMI |

There is a mini HDMI connector on the Raspberry Pi Zero. In order to connect it to an HDMI monitor you'll need a mini HDMI to standard HDMI adapter or cable. You can also buy a cable that has a mini HDMI connector on one end and a regular HDMI connector on the other. Here is an image of the adapter:

To use this connector, simply connect the adapter to your Raspberry Pi Zero, then the cable with the regular HDMI connections to the adapter and your TV or monitor that has an HDMI input connector. HDMI monitors are relatively new but if you have a monitor that has a DVI input, you can buy relatively inexpensive adapters that provide an interface between DVI and HDMI.

Don't be fooled by adapters that claim that they go from HDMI or DVI to VGA, or HDMI or DVI to S-video. These are two different kinds of signals: HDMI and DVI are digital standards, and VGA and S-video are analog standards. There are adapters that can do this, but they must contain circuitry and require power and they are significantly more expensive than any simple adapter.

You are almost ready to plug in the Raspberry Pi Zero. Connect your HDMI cable to your monitor and the Raspberry Pi Zero. Connect your USB hub to the Raspberry Pi Zero and connect your keyboard and mouse to the USB hub. Make sure that you connect all your devices before you power on the unit. Most operating systems support hot-swap of devices, which means you are able to connect a device after the system has been powered but this is a bit shaky. You should always cycle power when you connect new hardware. Here is a picture of everything connected:

The USB connectors are connected to USB power adapters. Even though your hardware configuration is complete, you'll still need to complete the next section to power on the device. So, let's figure out how to install an operating system.

Installing the operating system

Now that your hardware is ready, you need to download and image an operating system to a microSD card. The Raspberry Pi Zero provides a lot of different choices. You'll stick with Linux, an open-source version of Unix, on your Raspberry Pi Zero. Linux, unlike Windows, Android, or iOS, is not tightly controlled by a single company. It is a grassroots effort from a wide community, mostly open-source and, while it is available for free, it grows and develops a bit more chaotically.

A number of different versions of Linux have emerged, each built on a core set of similar capabilities referred to as the Linux kernel. These core capabilities are all based on the Linux specification. However, they are packaged slightly differently, and developed, supported, and packaged by different organizations. The Raspberry Pi community has become standardized on **Raspbian**, a **Debian** distribution of Linux for the Raspberry Pi. So, you are going to install and run Raspbian on your Raspberry Pi Zero.

The newest version of Debian is called **Jessie**, after the cowgirl in Toy Story®. This is the naming convention for Debian and you need to download this version of Raspbian.

You can purchase a card that has Raspbian installed or you can download it onto your personal computer and then install it on the card. To download a distribution, you need to decide if you are going to use a Windows computer to download and create an SD card, a MAC OS X, or a Linux machine. I'll give brief instructions for Windows and Linux machines here.

 For directions on the MAC OS X, go to: http://www. raspberrypi.org/documentation/installation/ installing-images/mac.md.

Firstly, you need to download an image. This part of the process is similar for both Windows and Linux. Open a browser window. Go to the Raspberry Pi organization's website, https://www.raspberrypi.org/ and select the **Downloads** selection at the top of the page. This will give you a variety of download choices. Go to the **Raspbian** section, and select the .zip file just to the right of the image identifier. You need the latest version, but not the lite one. This will download an archived file that has the image for your Raspbian operating system. Note the default username and password; you'll need them later.

If you're using Windows, you'll need to unzip the file using an archiving program like 7-Zip available at `http://www.7-zip.org/`. This will leave you with a file that has the `.img` extension, a file that can be imaged onto your card. Next, you need a program that can write the image to the card. I use Image Writer for Windows. You can find a link to this program at the top of the download section on the `https://www.raspberrypi.org/` website. Plug your card into the PC, run this program, and you should see this:

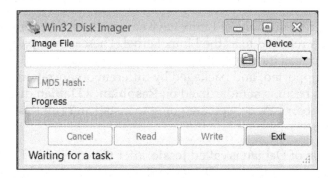

Select the device card and download the image; it should look something like this:

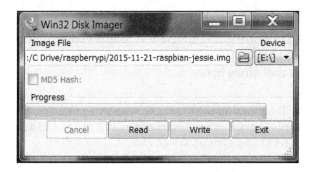

Then, click on the **Write** button. This will take some time, perhaps as long as 15 minutes but, when it is complete, exit the program and you'll have your microSD card with the image.

If you are using Linux, you need to un-archive the file and then write it to the card. You can do all of this with one command. However, you do need to find the `/dev` device label for your card. You can do this with the `ls -la /dev/sd*` command. If you run this before you plug in your card, you might see something like the following screenshot:

```
richard@vicki-automated: ~
richard@vicki-automated:~$ ls -la /dev/sd*
brw-rw---- 1 root disk 8, 0 Jul  4 10:34 /dev/sda
brw-rw---- 1 root disk 8, 1 Jul  4 10:34 /dev/sda1
brw-rw---- 1 root disk 8, 2 Jul  4 10:34 /dev/sda2
brw-rw---- 1 root disk 8, 5 Jul  4 10:34 /dev/sda5
richard@vicki-automated:~$
```

After plugging in your card, you might see something like the following screenshot:

```
richard@vicki-automated: ~
richard@vicki-automated:~$ ls -la /dev/sd*
brw-rw---- 1 root disk 8,  0 Jul  4 10:34 /dev/sda
brw-rw---- 1 root disk 8,  1 Jul  4 10:34 /dev/sda1
brw-rw---- 1 root disk 8,  2 Jul  4 10:34 /dev/sda2
brw-rw---- 1 root disk 8,  5 Jul  4 10:34 /dev/sda5
brw-rw---- 1 root disk 8, 16 Jul 11 09:50 /dev/sdb
brw-rw---- 1 root disk 8, 17 Jul 11 09:50 /dev/sdb1
brw-rw---- 1 root disk 8, 18 Jul 11 09:50 /dev/sdb2
richard@vicki-automated:~$
```

Note that your card is at sdb. Now go to the directory in which you downloaded the archived image file and use the following command:

```
sudo dd if=2015-11-21-raspbian-jessie.img  of=/dev/sdX
```

The 2015-11-21-raspbian-jessie.img command will be replaced by the image file that you downloaded and /dev/sdX will be replaced by your card ID, in this example /dev/sdb. Be careful to specify the correct device as this can overwrite the data on any of your drives. Also, this may take a few minutes. Once the file is written, eject the card and you are ready to plug it into the board and apply the power.

Make sure that your Raspberry Pi Zero is unplugged and install the SD card into the slot. Then power the device. After the device boots, you should get the following screen:

You are up and running!

 Note that, if you use a powered USB hub, it might provide enough power to your Raspberry Pi, however, in some circumstances it might not be able to provide all the power you need. I strongly suggest you use different power sources, one for your Raspberry Pi Zero and one for your hub.

You are going to do one more thing to finalize your configuration. To do this you need to go into the raspi-config application. So, open a terminal window by clicking the icon in the upper left corner that looks like a small computer screen.

Now, type in sudo raspi-config. You should see this application on your screen:

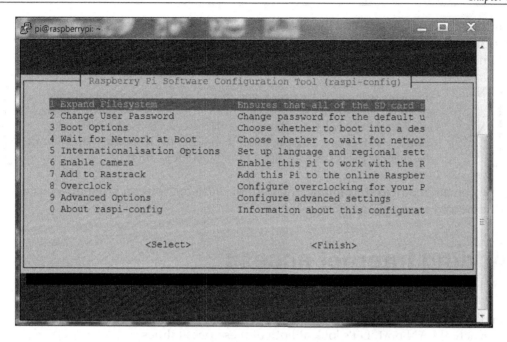

You need to expand the filesystem to take up the entire card. Select **1 Expand Filesystem**, hit the *Enter* key and you'll see the following screen:

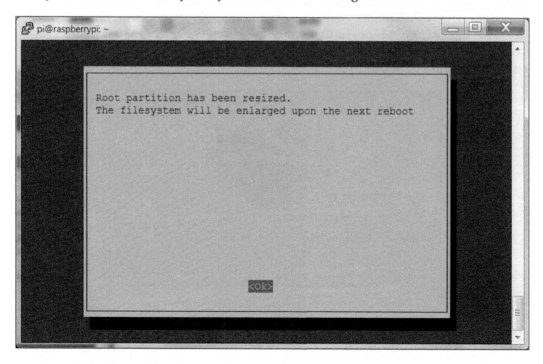

Hit *Enter* once again and you'll go back to the main configuration screen. Now, hit the *Tab* key until you are positioned over the **<Finish>** selection and then hit *Enter*. Then hit *Enter* again so that you can reboot your Raspberry Pi Zero.

> If you are using a US keyboard, you may need to edit the keyboard file for your keyboard to use nano effectively. To do this, use the dropdown menu in the upper left hand corner of the screen, choose **Preferences | Mouse and Keyboard Settings** and then select the **Keyboard** tab. You can then choose the correct keyboard for your configuration.

Now you are ready to start interacting with the system! You can bring up a terminal window and start typing commands.

Adding Internet access

The Raspberry Pi Zero does not have a LAN connection. To connect the Raspberry Pi Zero to the Internet, you have two choices. You can establish a wireless LAN connection or you can connect by using a USB to LAN adapter if you want to connect to an actual LAN port. Let's look at both of these possibilities.

If you are going to connect wirelessly, make sure that you have a wireless access point available. You'll also need a wireless device. The official Raspberry Pi Foundation markets a device itself, but other brands also work. See `http://elinux.org/RPi_USB_Wi-Fi_Adapters` to identify the wireless devices that have been verified to work with the Raspberry Pi Zero. Here is one that is available at many online electronics outlets:

You'll also need to connect a powered USB hub for this process, so that you can access both the keyboard and mouse, as well as the USB wireless LAN device. Now, connect the device to the powered hub.

Boot the system and then edit the `wpa_supplicant.conf` file by typing `sudo nano /etc/wpa_supplicant/wpa_supplicant.conf`. You need to change it to look like this:

The wpa-ssid and wpa-psk values here must, of course, match what your wireless access point requires. Reboot and your device should be connected to your wireless network. You'll know if it is connected by looking in the upper right hand corner of the screen where you should see the following:

You can now download any additional functionality you'll want to install from the Internet.

If you want to connect to an actual LAN cabled connection you need a device that goes from USB to LAN. This site http://elinux.org/RPi_USB_Ethernet_adapters lists a number of different possibilities. Here is an image of one such device:

Connecting the Raspberry Pi Zero in this way is actually amazingly easy. Simply plug the USB to LAN adapter into the powered USB hub, connect an active LAN cable and you should then have Internet access.

Accessing your Raspberry Pi Zero from your host PC

Once you have established an Internet network connection with your device, you can access it from your host computer. There are three ways to access your system from your remote computer:

- The first is through a terminal interface called **SSH**.

- The second way is by using a program called **VNC server**. This allows you to open a graphical user interface remotely which mirrors the graphical user interface on the Raspberry Pi.

- Finally, you can transfer files through a program called **WinSCP**, which is custom-made for this purpose. You can use a program called **SCP** for Linux.

So, firstly, make sure that your basic system is up and working. Open a terminal window and check the IP address of your unit. You're going to need this however you communicate with the system. Do this by using the `ifconfig` command. It should produce the following screenshot:

You need `inet addr`, which is shown in the third line of the preceding screenshot to contact your board through the Ethernet. If you are using a wireless device to gain access to the Internet, your `ifconfig` will look like this:

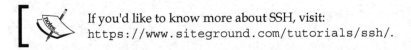

```
         pi@raspberrypi: ~
pi@raspberrypi ~ $ ifconfig
lo        Link encap:Local Loopback
          inet addr:127.0.0.1  Mask:255.0.0.0
          UP LOOPBACK RUNNING  MTU:65536  Metric:1
          RX packets:0 errors:0 dropped:0 overruns:0 frame:0
          TX packets:0 errors:0 dropped:0 overruns:0 carrier:0
          collisions:0 txqueuelen:0
          RX bytes:0 (0.0 B)  TX bytes:0 (0.0 B)

wlan0     Link encap:Ethernet  HWaddr 74:da:38:0c:f8:49
          inet addr:10.10.0.31  Bcast:10.10.0.255  Mask:255.255.255.0
          UP BROADCAST RUNNING MULTICAST  MTU:1500  Metric:1
          RX packets:98 errors:0 dropped:111 overruns:0 frame:0
          TX packets:130 errors:0 dropped:0 overruns:0 carrier:0
          collisions:0 txqueuelen:1000
          RX bytes:13798 (13.4 KiB)  TX bytes:20497 (20.0 KiB)

pi@raspberrypi ~ $
```

The `inet addr` associated with the `wlan0` connection, in this case `10.10.0.31`, is the address you will use to access your Raspberry Pi.

You also need an SSH terminal program running on your remote computer. An SSH terminal is a **Secure Shell (SSH)** connection, which simply means that you'll be able to access your board and give it commands by typing them into your remote computer. The response from the Raspberry Pi Zero will appear in the remote computer terminal window.

> If you'd like to know more about SSH, visit:
> `https://www.siteground.com/tutorials/ssh/`.

If you are running Microsoft Windows, you can download an alternative application. My personal favorite is **PuTTY**. It is free and does a very good job of saving your configuration so that you don't have to type it in every time. Type `putty` in a search engine and you'll soon come to a page that supports a download or you can go to `http://www.putty.org/`.

Download PuTTY to your Microsoft Windows machine. Then, run `putty.exe`. You should see a configuration window which looks something like the following screenshot:

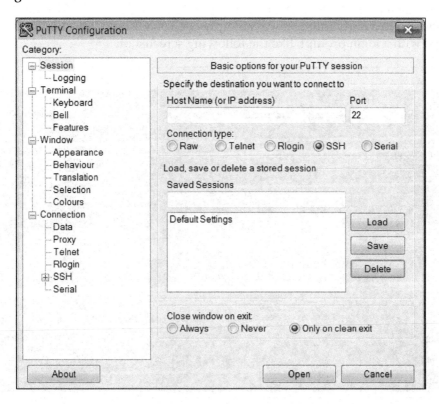

Type the `inet addr` from the previous page in the **Host Name** space and make sure that the **SSH** selection is selected. You may want to save this configuration under Raspberry Pi so that you can reload it each time.

When you click on **Open**, the system will try to open a terminal window onto your Raspberry Pi through the LAN connection. The first time you do this, you will get a warning about an RSA key as the two computers don't know about each other. Windows therefore complains that a computer that it doesn't know is about to be connected in a fairly intimate way. Simply click on **OK** and you should get a terminal with a login prompt, like the following screenshot:

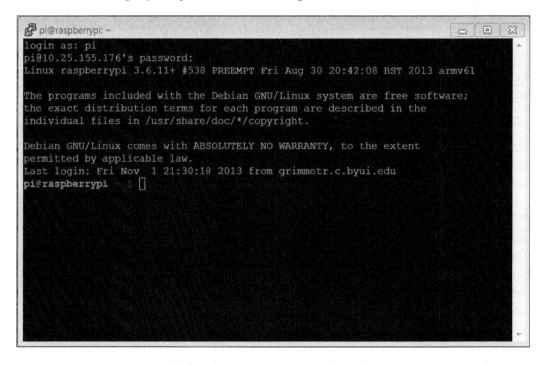

Now you can log in and issue commands to your Raspberry Pi Zero. If you'd like to do this from a Linux machine, the process is even simpler. Bring up a terminal window and then type ssh pi@xxx.xxx.xxx.xxx where the xxx.xxx.xxx.xxx is the inet addr of your device. This will then bring you to the login screen of your Raspberry Pi Zero, which should look similar to the preceding screenshot.

SSH is a really useful tool to communicate with your Raspberry Pi Zero. However, sometimes you need a graphical look at your system and you don't necessarily want to connect to a display. You can get this on your remote computer by using an application called **vncserver**. You'll need to install a version of this on your Raspberry Pi Zero by typing sudo apt-get install tightvncserver in a terminal window on your Raspberry Pi Zero. This is a perfect opportunity to use SSH, by the way.

Tightvncserver is an application that allows you to view your complete Raspberry Pi Zero remotely. Once you have it installed, you need to start the server by typing `vncserver` in a terminal window on the Raspberry Pi Zero. You will then be prompted for a password, then be prompted to verify the password, and then asked if you'd like to have a view-only password. Remember the password that you entered, you'll need it to log in via a VNC Viewer remotely.

You need a VNC Viewer application for your remote computer. On my Windows system, I use an application called **RealVNC**. When I start the application, it gives me the following screenshot:

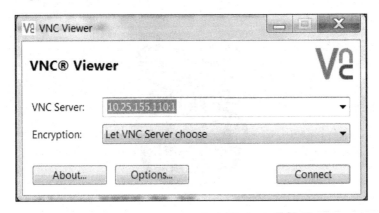

Enter the **VNC Server** address, which is the IP address of your Raspberry Pi Zero, and click on **Connect**. You will see a pop-up window, as shown in the following screenshot:

Type in the password that you just entered while starting vncserver and you should then get a graphical view of your Raspberry Pi that looks like the following screenshot:

You can now access all of the capabilities of your system, although they may be slower if you are doing a graphics-intense data transfer.

There are ways to make vncserver start automatically on boot. I have not used them; I prefer to type the vncserver command from an SSH application when I want the application running. This keeps your running applications to a minimum and, more importantly, presents fewer security risks. If you want to start yours each time you boot, there are several places on the Internet that show you how to configure this. Try the following website: http://www.havetheknowhow.com/ Configure-the-server/Run-VNC-on-boot.html.

To view this Raspberry Pi desktop from a remote Linux computer, which is running Ubuntu for example, you can type `sudo apt-get install xtightvncviewer`, then start it by using `xtightvncviewer 10.25.155.110:1` and supplying the chosen password.

Linux has viewers with graphical interfaces such as **Remmina Remote Desktop Client** (select the **VNC-Virtual Network Computing** protocol), which might be used instead of `xtightvncviewer`. Here is a screenshot of the **Remote Desktop Viewer**:

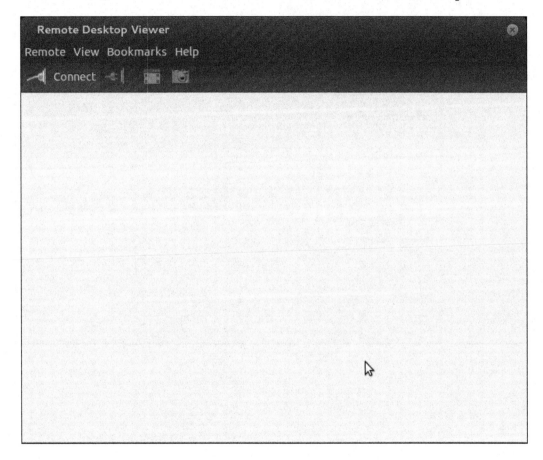

Make sure that vncserver is running on the Raspberry Pi Zero. The easiest way to do this is to log in using SSH and run vncserver at the prompt. Now, click on **Connect** on the **Remote Desktop Viewer**. Fill in the screen as follows, under the **Protocol** selection, choose **VNC**, and you should see the following screenshot:

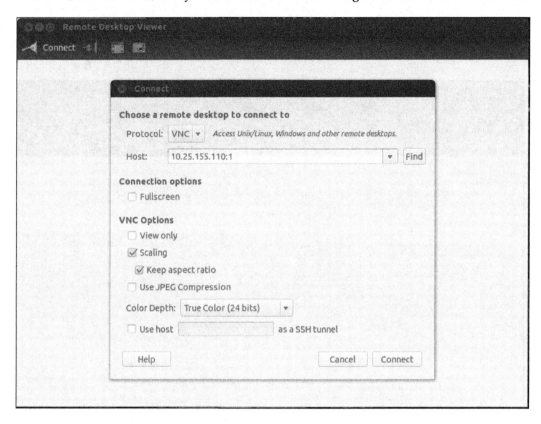

Now, enter the **Host** Internet address, making sure that you include a `:1` at the end and then click on **Connect**. You'll need to enter the vncserver password you set up, as shown in the following screenshot:

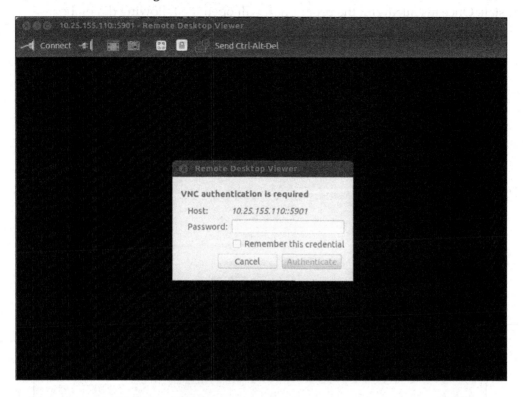

Now you should be able to see the graphical screen of the Raspberry Pi. To access the Raspberry Pi Zero graphically from a Mac or another Apple device, you can still use Real VNC Viewer, see `https://www.realvnc.com/products/` for more information.

The final piece of software that I like to use with Windows is a free application called **WinSCP**. To download and install this piece of software, go to `https://winscp.net/` and follow the instructions to download and install. Once installed, run the program. It will open the following dialog box:

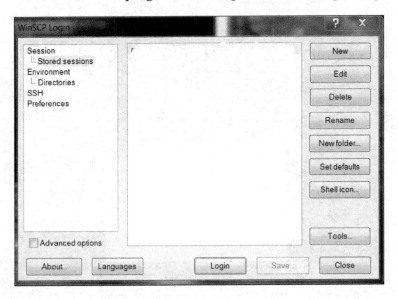

Click on **New** and you will get the following screenshot:

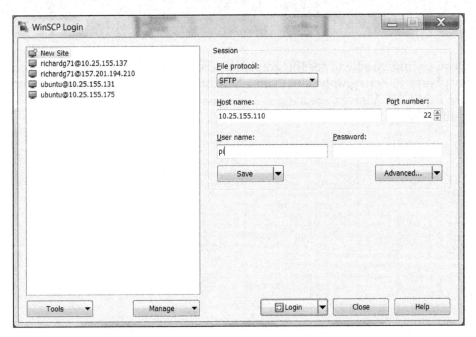

Here, you fill in the IP address in the **host name** tab, `pi` in the **user name** tab, and the password (not the vncserver password) in the **password** space. Click on **Login** and you should see a warning displayed, as shown in the following screenshot:

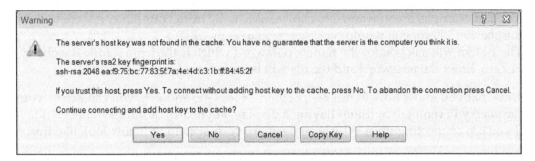

The host computer, again, doesn't know the remote computer. Click on **Yes** and the application will display the following screenshot:

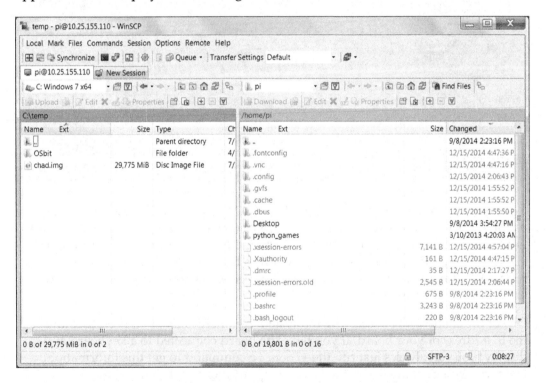

Now, you can drag and drop files from one system to the other. You can also do similar things with Linux by using the command line. To transfer a file to the remote Raspberry Pi, you can use the `scp file user@host.domain:path` command, where `file` is the filename, and `user@host.domain:path` is the location you want to copy it to. For example, if you wanted to copy `example.py` from your Linux system to the Raspberry Pi Zero, you would type `scp example.py pi@10.25.155.176:/home/pi/`. The system will ask you for the remote password which is the login for the Raspberry Pi Zero. Enter the password and the file will be transferred.

Now that you know how to use `ssh`, `tightvncserver`, and `scp`, you can access your Raspberry Pi remotely without having a display, keyboard, or mouse connected to it! If you are connecting via a WLAN connection, your system will now look like this:

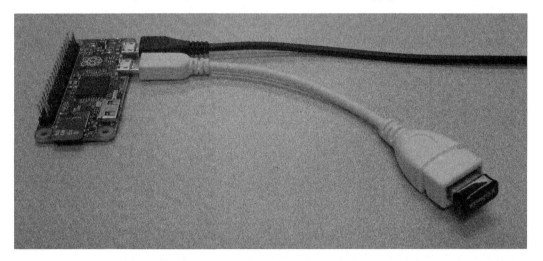

You only need to connect the power and the LAN, either with a cable or through wireless LAN. If you need to issue simple commands, connect through SSH. If you need a more complete set of graphical functionality, you can access this through `vncserver`. Finally, if you want to transfer files back and forth, you can use WinSCP from a Windows computer or `scp` from a Linux computer. Now you have the toolkit to build your first functionality.

One of the challenges of accessing the system remotely is that you need to know the IP address of your board. If you have the board connected to a keyboard and display, you can always just run the `ifconfig` command to get this information. However, you're going to use the board in applications in which you don't have this information. There is a way to discover this by using an IP scanner application. There are several available for free; on Windows, I use an application called **Advanced IP Scanner**, available at `www.advanced-ip-scanner.com/`. When you start the program, it looks like the following screenshot:

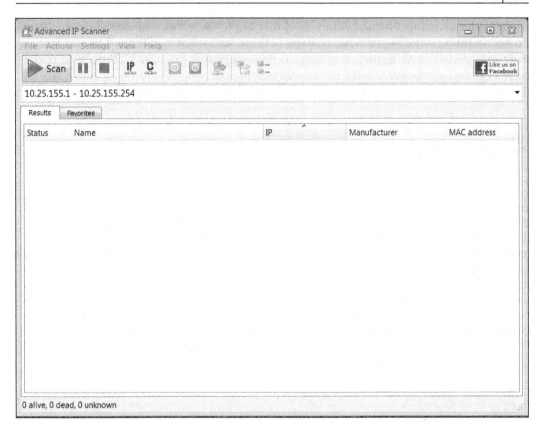

Clicking on the **Scan** selector scans for all the devices connected to the network. You can also do this in Linux; one application for IP scanning in Linux is called **Nmap**. To install Nmap, type `sudo apt-get install nmap`. To run Nmap, type `sudo nmap -sp 10.25.155.1/154` and the scanner will scan the addresses from `10.25.155.1` to `10.25.155.154`.

 For more information on Nmap, see: `:http://www.linux.com/learn/ tutorials/290879-beginners-guide-to-nmap`.

These scanners let you know which addresses are being used and this should allow you to see your Raspberry Pi address without typing `ipconfig`.

Your system has lots of capabilities. Feel free to play around with the system — try to get an understanding of what is already there and what you'll need to add from a software perspective. Remember, there is limited power on your USB port, so make sure that you are familiar with the power needs of accessories plugged into your Raspberry Pi. You may very well need to use a powered USB hub for many projects.

Summary

Congratulations! You've completed the first stage of your journey. You have your Raspberry Pi Zero up and working. No gathering dust in the bin for this piece of hardware. It is now ready to start connecting to all sorts of interesting devices, in all sorts of interesting ways. You have, by now, installed a Raspbian operating system, learned how to connect all the appropriate peripherals, and even mastered how to access the system remotely so that the only connections you need are a power supply cable and a LAN cable.

Now, you are ready to start commanding your Raspberry Pi Zero to do something. The next chapter will introduce you to the Linux operating system and the Emacs text editor. It will also show you some basic programming concepts in both the Python and C/C++ programming languages. Then, you'll be ready to add open source software to inexpensive hardware and start building your robotics projects.

2
Programming Raspberry Pi Zero

Now that your system is up and running, your Raspberry Pi Zero is ready to do something. This will require you to either create your own programs or edit someone else's programs. In this chapter, you'll learn how to edit a file to create a program that can run on Raspberry Pi Zero.

In this chapter, we will cover the following topics:

- Basic Linux commands and navigating the filesystem on Raspberry Pi Zero
- Creating, editing, and saving files on Raspberry Pi Zero
- Creating and running Python programs on Raspberry Pi Zero
- Some of the basic programming constructs in Python on Raspberry Pi Zero

You can create and run the programs discussed in this chapter by connecting a keyboard, a mouse, and a monitor to Raspberry Pi Zero, or remotely logging in using vncserver or SSH.

Powering up Raspberry Pi Zero with Linux

After completing the tasks discussed in *Chapter 1*, *Getting Started with Raspberry Pi Zero*, you'll have a working Raspberry Pi Zero that is running a version of Linux called Raspbian. So, power up your Raspberry Pi Zero and log in using a valid username and password. If you are going to log in remotely through SSH or vncserver, go ahead and establish the connection now. First, you'll take a quick tour of Linux. This will not be extensive, but you will just walk through some of the basic commands.

Once you have logged in, open up a terminal window. If you are logging in using a keyboard, mouse, and monitor, or using vncserver, you'll find the terminal by selecting the **Terminal** application on icon set selection at the top of the screen, as shown in the following screenshot:

If you are using SSH, you will already be in the terminal emulator program. Either way, the terminal should look something similar to the following screenshot:

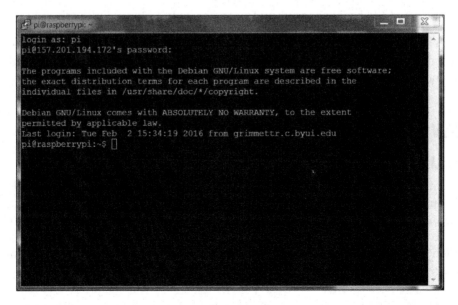

Your cursor is at the Command Prompt. Unlike Microsoft Windows or Mac's OS, with Linux, most of our work will be done by actually typing commands in the command line. So, let's try a few commands. When you type ls, you should be able to see the result similar to the following screenshot:

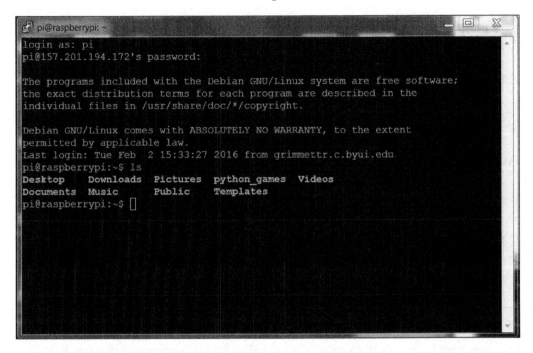

In Linux, the ls command lists all the files and directories in our current directory. You can tell the different file types and directories apart because they are normally in different colors. You can also use ls -l to see more information about the files.

You can move around the directory structure by issuing the cd (change directory) command. For example, if you want to see what is in the Desktop directory, type cd Desktop. If you issue the ls command now, you should see something similar to the following screenshot:

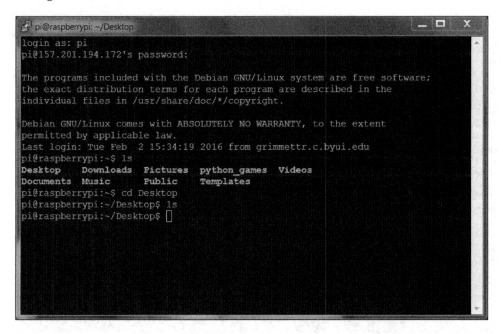

This directory is empty; it doesn't have any files. The cd command changes the directory. You could have typed cd /home/pi/Desktop and received exactly the same result; this is because you were in the /home/pi directory, which is the directory where you always start when you first log in to the system.

If you ever want to see which directory you are in, simply type pwd, which stands for present working directory. If you do that, you will get the result, which is similar to the following screenshot:

The result of running the pwd command is /home/pi/Desktop. Now, you can use two different shortcuts to navigate back to the default directory. The first is to type cd .. on the terminal; this will take you to the directory just above the current directory in the hierarchy. Then type pwd; you should see the following screenshot as a result:

The other way to get back to the home directory is by typing cd ~; this will always return you to your home directory. You can also type cd to return to your home directory. If you were to do this from the Desktop directory and then type pwd, you would see the following screenshot as the result:

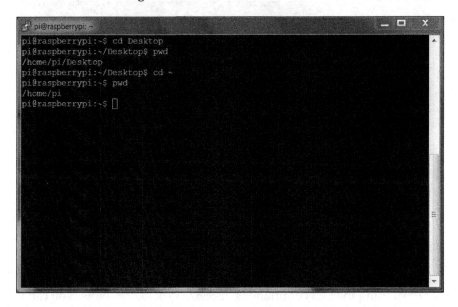

You can go to a specific directory using its entire pathname. In this case, if you want to go to the /home/pi/Desktop directory from anywhere in the filesystem, simply type cd /home/pi/Desktop.

There are a number of other Linux commands that you might find useful as you program. The following is a table with some of the most useful commands:

Linux commands	What it does
ls	This command lists all the files and directories in the current directory by just their names.
rm filename	This command deletes the file specified by filename.
mv filename1 filename2	This command renames filename1 to filename2.

Linux commands	What it does
`cp filename1 filename2`	This command copies `filename1` to `filename2`.
`mkdir directoryname`	This command creates a directory with the name specified by `directoryname`; this will be made in the current directory unless specified otherwise.
`clear`	This command clears the current terminal window.
`sudo`	If you type the `sudo` command at the beginning of any command, it will execute that command as the super user. This may be required if the command or program you are trying to execute needs the permission of the super user. If, at any point, you type a command or the name of the program you want to run and the result seems to suggest that the command does not exist or that permission is denied, try doing it again with `sudo` at the beginning.

Now, you can play around with the commands and look at your system and the files that are available to you. But, be careful! Linux is not like Windows; the default behavior is to not warn you if you try to delete or replace a file.

Creating, editing, and saving files

Now that you can log in and move easily between directories and see your files, you'll want to be able to edit those files. To do this, you'll need a program that allows you to edit the characters in a file. If you are used to working on Microsoft Windows, you have probably used programs such as Microsoft Notepad, WordPad, or Word to do this. These programs are not available in Linux. There are several other choices for editors, all of which are free. In this chapter, you will use an editing program called **Emacs**. Other possibilities are programs such as nano, vi, vim, and gedit. Programmers have strong feelings about which editor to use, so if you already have a favorite, you can skip this section.

 If you want to use nano as an editor, it is already available on the Raspbian distribution. For more information on nano, see http://www.nano-editor.org/.

If you want to use Emacs, download and install it by typing `sudo apt-get install emacs`. Once installed, you can run Emacs simply by typing `emacs filename`, where `filename` is the name of the file you want to edit. If the file does not exist, Emacs will create it. The following screenshot shows what you will see if you type `emacs example.py` on the prompt:

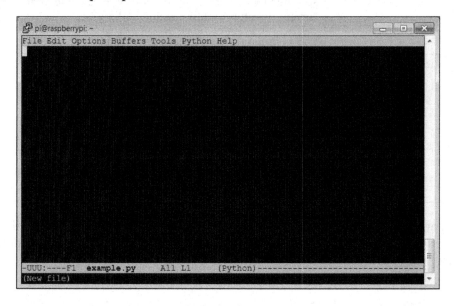

Note that, unlike Windows, Linux doesn't automatically assign file extensions; it is up to you to specify the kind of file you want to create. The Emacs editor also indicates, in the lower-left corner of the screen, that you have opened a new file. Now, if you are using Emacs in the Raspbian GUI interface, either because you have a monitor, keyboard, and mouse hooked up or because you are running vncserver, you can use the mouse in much the same way as you do in Microsoft Word.

However, if you are running Emacs from SSH, you won't have the mouse available. So you'll need to navigate the file using the cursor keys. You'll also have to use some keystroke commands to save your file, as well as accomplish a number of other tasks that you would normally use the mouse to select. For example, when you are ready to save the file, you must press *Ctrl* + *X* and *Ctrl* + *S* and that will save the file under the current filename. When you want to quit Emacs, you must press *Ctrl* + *X* and *Ctrl* + *C*. This will stop Emacs and return you to the Command Prompt.

The following are some Emacs keystroke commands that you might find useful:

Emacs commands	What it does
Ctrl + X and *Ctrl + S*	**Save**: This command saves the current file.
Ctrl + X and *Ctrl + C*	**Quit**: This command makes you exit Emacs and return to the command prompt.
Ctrl + K	**Kill**: This command erases the current line.
Ctrl + _	**Undo**: This command undoes the last action.
Left-click on the text you wish to copy, then place the cursor cursor at the place you want to paste then right-click	**Cut and paste**: If you select the text you want to paste by clicking the mouse, move the cursor to where you want to paste the code and then right-click on it; the code will be pasted in that location.

Now that you have the capability to edit files, you'll use this capability to create programs in the next section.

Creating and running Python programs

Now that you are ready to begin programming, you'll need to choose a language. There are many available, such as C, C++, Java, Python, Perl, and a great deal of other possibilities. I'm going to initially introduce you to Python for two reasons: it is a simple language that is intuitive and very easy to use, and it uses a lot of the open source functionality of the robotics world. We'll also cover a bit of C/C++ in this chapter, as some features are only available in C/C++. However, it makes sense to start with Python. To work through the examples in this section, you'll need a version of Python installed. Fortunately, the basic Raspbian system has one already, so you are ready to begin.

We are only going to cover some of the very basic concepts here. If you are new to programming, there are a number of different websites that provide interactive tutorials. If you'd like to practice some of the basic programming concepts in Python using these tutorials, visit `https://www.codeacademy.com` or `http://www.learnpython.org/` or `https://docs.python.org` and give it a try.

In this section, we'll cover how to create and run a Python file. It turns out that Python can be used interactively, so you can type in the commands one at a time. Using it interactively is extremely helpful when you are getting acquainted with the language features and modules. But you want to use Python to create programs, so you are going to type in your commands using Emacs and then run them in the command line by invoking Python. Let's get started.

Open an example Python file by typing `emacs example.py`. Now, let's put some code in the file. Start with the code shown in the following screenshot:

```
pi@raspberrypi: ~
File Edit Options Buffers Tools Python Help
a = input("Input value: ")
b = input("Input second value: ")
c = a + b
print c
```

Let's go through the code to see what is happening. The code lines are as follows:

- `a = input("Input value: ")`: One of the basic purposes of a program is to get input from the user; `input` allows us to do that. The data will be input by the user and stored in a. The prompt `Input value:` will be shown to the user.

- `b = input("Input second value: ")`: This data will also be input by the user and stored in b. The prompt `Input second value:` will be shown to the user.

- `c = a + b`: This is an example of something you can do with the data; in this example, you can add a and b.

- `print c`: Another basic purpose of our program is to print out results. The `print` command prints out the value of c.

This code is written using Python 2. If you are using Python 3, you will need to change your `print` to `print(c)`. For other changes that might be required, go to `http://learntocodewith.me/programming/python/python-2-vs-python-3/`.

Once you have created your program, save it (using *Ctrl + X* and *Ctrl + S*) and quit Emacs (using *Ctrl + X* and *Ctrl + C*). Now, from the command line, run your program by typing `python example.py`. The result you see should be similar to the following screenshot:

You can also run the program from the command line without typing `python example.py` by adding the `#!/usr/bin/python` line to the program. Then the program looks similar to the following screenshot:

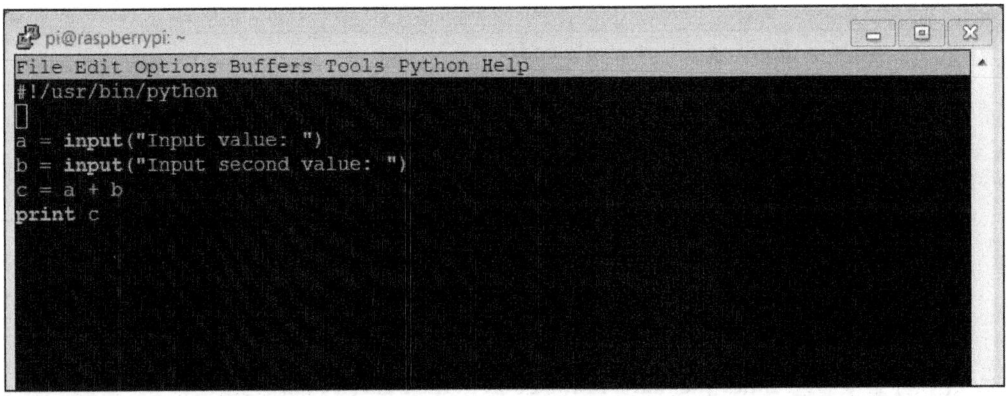

Adding `#!/usr/bin/python` as the first line, simply makes this file available for us to execute from the command line. Once you have saved the file and exited Emacs, type `chmod +x example.py`. This will change the file's execution permissions, so the computer will now accept and execute it.

You should be able to simply type `./example.py` and see the program run, as shown in the following screenshot:

```
pi@raspberrypi:~$ python example.py
Input value: 5
Input second value: 2
7
pi@raspberrypi:~$ emacs example.py
pi@raspberrypi:~$ chmod +x example.py
pi@raspberrypi:~$ ./example.py
Input value: 6
Input second value: 7
13
pi@raspberrypi:~$ []
```

Note that if you simply type `example.py`, the system will not find the executable file. Here, the file has not been registered with the system, so you have to give the system a path to it. In this case, `./` is the current directory.

Downloading the example code

You can download the example code files for this book from your account at http://www.packtpub.com. If you purchased this book elsewhere, you can visit http://www.packtpub.com/support and register to have the files e-mailed directly to you.

You can download the code files by following these steps:

- Log in or register to our website using your e-mail address and password.
- Hover the mouse pointer on the **SUPPORT** tab at the top.
- Click on **Code Downloads & Errata**.
- Enter the name of the book in the **Search** box.
- Select the book for which you're looking to download the code files.
- Choose from the drop-down menu where you purchased this book from.
- Click on **Code Download**.

Once the file is downloaded, please make sure that you unzip or extract the folder using the latest version of:

- WinRAR/7-Zip for Windows
- Zipeg/iZip/UnRarX for Mac
- 7-Zip/PeaZip for Linux

Basic programming constructs on Raspberry Pi Zero

Now that you know how to enter and run a simple Python program on Raspberry Pi Zero, let's look at some more complex programming tools. Specifically, we'll cover what to do when we want to determine the instructions to execute and how to loop our code to do that more than once. I'll give a brief introduction on how to use libraries in the Python version 2.7 code and how to organize statements into functions. Finally, we'll very briefly cover object-oriented code organization.

 Indentation in Python is very important; it will specify which group of statements is associated with a given loop or decision set, so watch your indentation carefully.

The if statement

As you have seen in previous examples, your programs normally start by executing the first line of code and then continue with the following lines until the program runs out of code. But, what if you want to decide between two different courses of action? We can do this in Python using an `if` statement. The following screenshot shows some example code:

```
pi@raspberrypi: ~
File Edit Options Buffers Tools Python Help
#!/usr/bin/python

a = input("Input value: ")
b = input("Input second value: ")
if a > b:
    c = a - b
else:
    c = b - a
print c
```

The following are the details of the code shown in the previous screenshot:

- `#!/usr/bin/python`: This is included so that you can make your program executable.

- `a = input("Input value: ")`: The data will be input by the user and stored in `a`. `b = input("Input second value: ")`: This data will also be input by the user and stored in `b`.

- `if a > b:`: This is an `if` statement. The expression evaluated in this case is `a > b`. If it is `True`, the program will execute the next one or more statements that are indented; in this case, `c = a - b`. If not, it will skip that statement.

- `else:`:The `else` statement is an optional part of the command. If the expression in the `if` statement is evaluated as `False`, the indented statements after the `else:` statement will be executed; in this case, `c = b - a`.

- `print c`: Another basic purpose of our program is to print out results. The `print` command prints out the value of `c`.

You can run the previous program a couple of times, checking both the `True` and `False` possibilities of the `if` expression, as shown in the following screenshot:

```
pi@raspberrypi: ~
pi@raspberrypi:~$ ./example.py
Input value: 5
Input second value: 2
3
pi@raspberrypi:~$ ./example.py
Input value: 3
Input second value: 8
5
pi@raspberrypi:~$ []
```

The while statement

Another useful construct is the `while` construct; it allows us to execute a set of statements over and over again until a specific condition has been met. The following screenshot shows a set of code that uses this construct:

```
pi@raspberrypi: ~
File Edit Options Buffers Tools Python Help
#!/usr/bin/python

a = 0
b = 1
while a != b:
    a = input("Input value: ")
    b = input("Input second value: ")
    c = a + b
    print c
```

The following are the details of the code shown in the previous screenshot:

- `#!/usr/bin/python`: This is included so you can make your program executable.

- `a = 0`: This line sets the value of variable a to 0. We'll need this only to make sure that we execute the loop at least once.

- `b = 1`: This line sets the value of the variable b to 1. We'll need this only to make sure that we execute the loop at least once.

- `while a != b:`: The expression a `!=` b (in this case, `!=` means not equal to) is verified. If it is `True`, the indented statements are executed. When the statement is evaluated as `False`, the program jumps to the statements (none in this example) after the indented section.

- `a = input("Input value: ")`: The data will be input by the user and stored in a.

- `b = input("Input second value: ")`: This data will also be input by the user and stored in b.

- `c = a + b`: The variable c is loaded with the sum of a and b.

- `print c`: The `print` command prints out the value of c.

Now you can run the program. Note that when you enter the same value for a and b, the program stops, as shown in the following screenshot:

```
pi@raspberrypi: ~
pi@raspberrypi:~$ ./example.py
Input value: 3
Input second value: 4
7
Input value: 5
Input second value: 5
10
pi@raspberrypi:~$ 
```

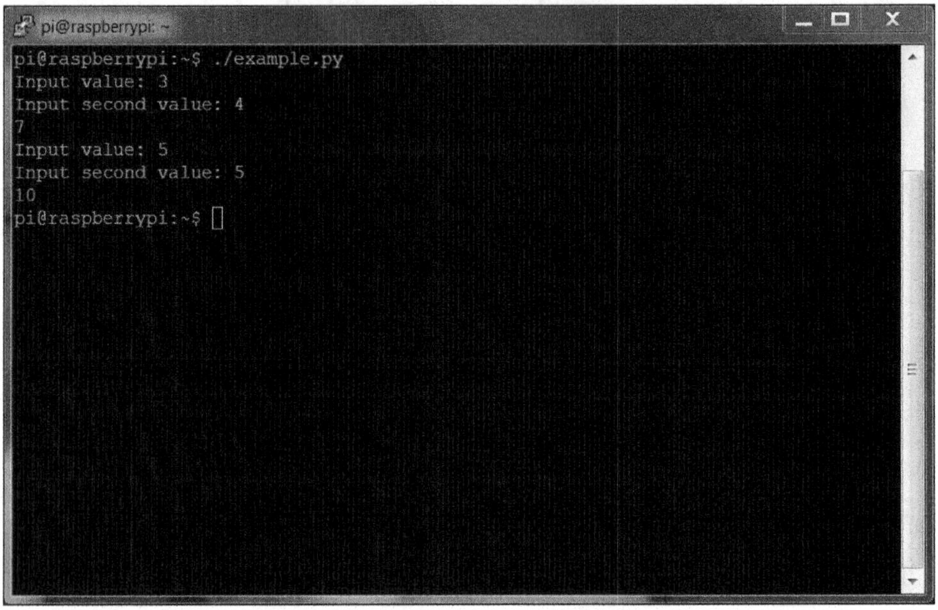

Working with functions

The next concept that we need to cover is how to put a set of statements into a function. We use functions to organize code and group sets of statements together when it makes sense to organize them in the same location. For example, if we have a specific calculation that we might want to perform many times, instead of copying the set of statements every time we want to perform it, we group them into a function. I'll use a fairly simple example here, but if the calculation takes a significant number of programming statements, you can see how that would make our code significantly easier to maintain, as we don't need to duplicate our code over and over. It can also make our code easier to read. The following screenshot shows the code:

```
pi@raspberrypi: ~                                          _ □ X
File Edit Options Buffers Tools Python Help
#!/usr/bin/python

def sum(a, b):
    c = a + b
    return c


d = input("Input value: ")
e = input("Input second value: ")
f = sum(d, e)
print f






-UU-:----F1   example.py     All L11   (Python) ------------------
Wrote /home/pi/example.py
```

The following is the explanation of the code from our previous example:

- `#!/usr/bin/python`: This is included so you can make your program executable.

- `def sum(a, b)::` This line defines a function named `sum`. The `sum` function takes `a` and `b` as arguments.

- `c = a + b`: Whenever this function is called, it will add the values in the variable `a` to the values in variable `b`.

- `return c`: When the function is executed, it will return variable `c` to the calling expression.

- `d = input("Input value: ")`: This data will also be input by the user and will be stored in `d`. The prompt `Input second value:` will be shown to the user.

- `e = input("Input second value: ")`: This data will also be input by the user and stored in `e`. The prompt `Input second value:` will be shown to the user.

- `f = sum(d, e)`: The function `sum` is called. The program then goes to the `sum` function and executes it. The value in variable `d` is copied to the variable `a` and the value in the variable `e` is copied to the variable `b`. The value is returned from the function and then stored in variable `f`.

- `print f`: The `print` command prints out the value of `f`.

The following screenshot is the result received when you run the code:

```
pi@raspberrypi: ~

pi@raspberrypi:~$ ./example.py
Input value: 6
Input second value: 3
9
pi@raspberrypi:~$
```

Libraries/modules in Python

The next topic we need to cover is how to add functionality to our programs using libraries/modules. Libraries or modules, as they are sometimes called in Python, include a functionality that someone else has created and that you want to add to your code. As long as the functionality exists and your system knows about it, you can include the library in the code.

So, let's modify our code again by adding the library, as shown in the following screenshot:

The following is a line-by-line description of the code:

- `#!/usr/bin/python`: This is included so that you can make your program executable.
- `import time`: This includes the `time` library. The `time` library includes a function that allows you to pause for a specified number of seconds.
- `d = input("Input value: ")`: This data will be input by the user and will be stored in `d`. The prompt `Input second value:` will be shown to the user.
- `time.sleep(2)`: This line calls the `sleep` function in the `time` library, which will cause a 2 second delay.
- `e = input("Input second value: ")`: This data will also be input by the user and will be stored in `b`. The prompt `Input second value:` will be shown to the user.
- `f = d + e`: The `f` variable is loaded with the value `d + e`.
- `print f`: The `print` command prints out the value of `f`.

The following screenshot shows the result after running the previous example code:

```
pi@raspberrypi:~$ ./example.py
Input value: 5
Input second value: 7
12
pi@raspberrypi:~$
```

Of course, this looks very similar to other results. But you will notice a pause between you entering the first value and the appearance of the second value.

Summary

In this chapter, you've learned how to interact with the Raspbian operating system using the command line and how to create and edit files using Emacs. You have also been exposed to both the Python and C programming languages. If this is your first experience with programming, don't be surprised if you are still very uneasy with programming in general, and if and while statements in particular. You probably felt just as uncomfortable during your first introduction to the English language, although you may not remember it.

It is always a bit difficult to try new things. However, I will try to give you explicit instructions on what to type so that you can be successful. There is one major challenge in working with computers. They always do exactly what you tell them to do and not necessarily what you want them to. So if you encounter problems, check several times to make sure that your code matches the example exactly. Now, on to some actual coding!

In the next chapter, you'll start writing code that will enable you to create amazing projects. You'll start by providing your system with the ability to speak and also listen to your commands.

3

Accessing the GPIO Pins on Raspberry Pi Zero

Now that you are familiar with Raspberry Pi Zero and also how to create, edit, and upload a program, this chapter will turn your focus to the hardware. You'll get the chance to learn how to connect and access, from the software, the capabilities of the Raspberry Pi GPIO pins.

In this chapter you'll learn:

- All about Raspberry Pi Zero's GPIO pins and what they can and can't do
- A very basic circuit and very simple programming examples of how to interface Raspberry Pi Zero's GPIO to produce a digital control signal
- A more complex example of how to interface Raspberry Pi Zero's GPIO with a sonar sensor
- An example of how to connect an I2C device to Raspberry Pi Zero

The GPIO capability of Raspberry Pi Zero

Raspberry Pi Zero was built to access the outside world. Much of this access is available through the GPIO pins. Let's start by detailing what the GPIO pins are and what they can do. Raspberry Pi Zero has 40 GPIO pins.

Here is a closeup of the 40 pins:

Here is a listing of the pins and their connection to the Raspberry Pi Zero:

Pin 1 3.3V	☐○	Pin 2 5V
Pin 3 GPIO2	○○	Pin 4 5V
Pin 5 GPIO3	○○	Pin 6 GND
Pin 7 GPIO4	○○	Pin 8 GPIO14
Pin 9 GND	○○	Pin 10 GPIO15
Pin 11 GPIO17	○○	Pin 12 GPIO18
Pin 13 GPIO27	○○	Pin 14 GND
Pin 15 GPIO22	○○	Pin 16 GPIO23
Pin 17 3.3V	○○	Pin 18 GPIO24
Pin 19 GPIO10	○○	Pin 20 GND
Pin 21 GPIO9	○○	Pin 22 GPIO25
Pin 23 GPIO11	○○	Pin 24 GPIO8
Pin 25 GND	○○	Pin 26 GPIO7
Pin 27 ID_SD	○○	Pin 28 ID_SC
Pin 29 GPIO5	○○	Pin 30 GND
Pin 31 GPIO6	○○	Pin 32 GPIO12
Pin 33 GPIO13	○○	Pin 34 GND
Pin 35 GPIO19	○○	Pin 36 GPIO16
Pin 37 GPIO26	○○	Pin 38 GPIO20
Pin 39 GND	○○	Pin 40 GPIO21

The purpose of some of these pins is very clear. Pins 1 and 17 are available to supply 3.3 volts, pins 2 and 4 supply 5 volts, and pins 9, 25, 39, 6, 14, 20, 30, and 34 are all connected to ground on Raspberry Pi Zero. The rest of the pins have various capabilities, which you'll learn in this chapter. Let's start with the pins that can be used to supply a simple DC signal to the outside world.

Simple GPIO digital voltage output

Perhaps the simplest connection that you can make to the GPIO on Raspberry Pi is to connect to a pin so that you can send a simple digital output voltage. To do this, you will use the GPIO IO pins to light up an LED. To be successful, you'll need four pieces of hardware: a solder-less breadboard, some jumper wires, an LED, and a resistor. Here are more details on these parts:

1. A breadboard is a simple device that lets you easily connect your various electronic parts. They come in various sizes, shapes, and colors. Here is a picture of such a breadboard:

They are available at many online outlets and hobby shops.

2.   Jumper wires are designed to connect your various electronics parts. These are specified by female or male ends, depending on the type of connection. Here is a picture of a male to female jumper wire, with the ends labeled:

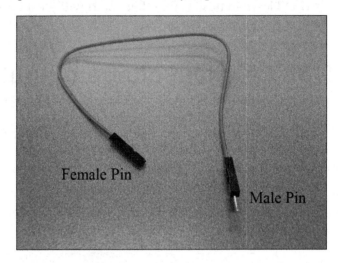

For these projects, you'll want some female to male jumper cables and some female to female jumper cables.

3.   A **Light Emitting Diode (LED)** is a small component with two leads that light up when a voltage is applied. They come in a wide variety of colors. If you want to buy them online, search for a 3 mm LED. They come in various colors. You can also get them at most electronics shops. Here is one:

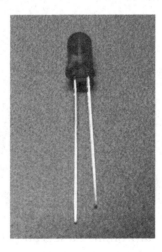

4. You'll also need a resistor to limit the current supplied to the LED. A 220-ohm resistor would be the right size. Again, you can get them online or at most electronics shops. Here is an image of a set of such resistors:

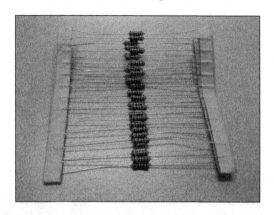

If you get two each of LED and resistor, you can exercise several of the GPIO IO pins. Now that you have all the bits and bobs, let's build your first hardware project. Before you plug anything in, lets look at the breadboard for a moment so that you can understand how you are going to use it to make connections. You'll be plugging your wires into the holes on the breadboard. The holes on the breadboard are connected in a unique way to make the connections you desire.

In the middle of the board, the holes are connected across the board. So if you plug in the wire with another wire in the hole right next to it, these two wires will be connected, like this:

The two rows on each side of the board are generally designed to provide power, so they are connected up and down. Connect pin 2, 3 volts, to the + connection and pin 6, GND, to the + and – rows of the breadboard, as shown:

Now you can place the electronic parts on the breadboard. Place the LEDs so that one wire is on one side of the middle split of the breadboard. The direction on the LED is important; make sure that the longer of the two wires is on the left-hand side of the hole.

Now place the resistors on the holes on one side of the LED, with the other lead connected to the GND row of the breadboard. The direction of the resistor does not make any difference. Your circuit should look similar to the following image:

Now you'll use the jumper wires to connect to Raspberry Pi Zero's GPIO pins. You'll connect to pin 13 (GPIO 27) and pin 15 (GPIO 22), as shown:

Choosing the right pins is important, as not all of the pins are available to output a GPIO voltage. Here is another view of the GPIO pins, labeled with some of the dedicated functions that have been assigned to them:

	Pin 1 3.3V ▢○ Pin 2 5V
I2C Interface	Pin 3 GPIO2 ○○ Pin 4 5V
	Pin 5 GPIO3 ○○ Pin 6 GND
	Pin 7 GPIO4 ○○ Pin 8 GPIO14 — **Serial Interface**
	Pin 9 GND ○○ Pin 10 GPIO15
	Pin 11 GPIO17 ○○ Pin 12 GPIO18
	Pin 13 GPIO27 ○○ Pin 14 GND
	Pin 15 GPIO22 ○○ Pin 16 GPIO23
	Pin 17 3.3V ○○ Pin 18 GPIO24
SPI Interface	Pin 19 GPIO10 ○○ Pin 20 GND
	Pin 21 GPIO9 ○○ Pin 22 GPIO25
	Pin 23 GPIO11 ○○ Pin 24 GPIO8 — **SPI Interface**
	Pin 25 GND ○○ Pin 26 GPIO7
EEPROM	Pin 27 ID_SD ○○ Pin 28 ID_SC
	Pin 29 GPIO5 ○○ Pin 30 GND
	Pin 31 GPIO6 ○○ Pin 32 GPIO12
	Pin 33 GPIO13 ○○ Pin 34 GND
	Pin 35 GPIO19 ○○ Pin 36 GPIO16
	Pin 37 GPIO26 ○○ Pin 38 GPIO20
	Pin 39 GND ○○ Pin 40 GPIO21

You'll learn more about the dedicated functions in this chapter and throughout the book. Now that the hardware is configured correctly, you'll need to add code to drive the LEDs.

Raspberry Pi Zero and LED code

To create the code, you'll now want to boot up, log in, and open a terminal window on Raspberry Pi Zero. You'll use Python to create a simple program to turn on and off the LEDs. Here is the code:

```
pi@raspberrypi: ~
File Edit Options Buffers Tools Python Help
#!/user/bin/python

import RPi.GPIO as io
import time

io.setmode(io.BCM)

led1 = 27
led2 = 22

io.setup(led1,io.OUT)
io.setup(led2,io.OUT)
while 1:
    io.output(led1, True)
    io.output(led2, True)
    time.sleep(1)
    io.output(led1, False)
    io.output(led2, False)
    time.sleep(1)

-UU-:----F1   led.py         All L1      (Python) --------------------------
For information about GNU Emacs and the GNU system, type C-h C-a.
```

Now enter the program. Lets go through the program line by line:

- `#!/usr/bin/python`: This line lets you run this program without having to type `python` before the filename. You'll learn how to do this at the end of these instructions.

- `import RPi.GPIO as io`: This lets you import the `RPi.GPIO` library, which will allow you to control the GPIO pins.

- `import time`: The `time` library provides several time-based functions. In this case, you'll use it to pause the program for a few seconds.

- `io.setmode(io.BCM)`: This sets the specification mode of the GPIO pins to Broadcom SOC channel number (BCM). This means that you will specify the GPIO numbers of the pins you want to control, instead of the actual physical pin numbers.

- `led1 = 27`: This assigns the value `27` to the `led1` variable.

- `led2 = 22`: This assigns the value `22` to the `led2` variable.

- `io.setup(led1, io.OUT)`: This sets the GPIO pin 27 to an output control.

- `io.setup(led2, io.OUT)`: This sets the GPIO pin 22 to an output control.

- `while 1:`: This puts you in a repeat-forever loop. To stop the program you'll want to press *Ctrl + C*.

- `io.output(led1, True)`: This will output a 3.3 volt signal on `led1` (this is GPIO 27).

- `io.output(led2, True)`: This will output a 3.3 volt signal on `led1` (this is GPIO 22).

- `time.sleep(1)`: This will pause a program for one second.

- `io.output(led1, False)`: This will output 0 volts on `led1` (this is GPIO 27).

- `io.output(led2, False)`: This will output 0 volts on `led2` (this is GPIO 22).

- `time.sleep(1)`: This pauses a program for one second.

Save the program under the name `led.py`. Now run the program by typing `python led.py`. You should see the two LEDs flash at one second intervals, as shown:

You've just completed your first hardware project with Raspberry Pi Zero!

Adding a sonar sensor

The basic circuit you just built is a wonderful start. Now you'll interface a more complex device, a sonar sensor, with Raspberry Pi Zero. Here is a picture of the sonar sensor that you'll add:

The device is an HC-SR04 and they are available at most online electronics retailers. Now let's connect the device to Raspberry Pi Zero. In order to do this, first let's look at the layout of the GPIO pins on Raspberry Pi Zero:

Pin 1 3.3V	□ ○	Pin 2 5V
Pin 3 GPIO2	○ ○	Pin 4 5V
Pin 5 GPIO3	○ ○	Pin 6 GND
Pin 7 GPIO4	○ ○	Pin 8 GPIO14
Pin 9 GND	○ ○	Pin 10 GPIO15
Pin 11 GPIO17	○ ○	Pin 12 GPIO18
Pin 13 GPIO27	○ ○	Pin 14 GND
Pin 15 GPIO22	○ ○	Pin 16 GPIO23
Pin 17 3.3V	○ ○	Pin 18 GPIO24
Pin 19 GPIO10	○ ○	Pin 20 GND
Pin 21 GPIO9	○ ○	Pin 22 GPIO25
Pin 23 GPIO11	○ ○	Pin 24 GPIO8
Pin 25 GND	○ ○	Pin 26 GPIO7
Pin 27 ID_SD	○ ○	Pin 28 ID_SC
Pin 29 GPIO5	○ ○	Pin 30 GND
Pin 31 GPIO6	○ ○	Pin 32 GPIO12
Pin 33 GPIO13	○ ○	Pin 34 GND
Pin 35 GPIO19	○ ○	Pin 36 GPIO16
Pin 37 GPIO26	○ ○	Pin 38 GPIO20
Pin 39 GND	○ ○	Pin 40 GPIO21

You'll need to connect to the 5 volt connection of the Raspberry Pi Zero, pin 2. You also need to connect to the GND, which is pin 6 on Raspberry Pi. Pin 16 (GPIO 23) is used as an output trigger pin and pin 18 (GPIO 24) as an input to time the echo from the sonar sensor.

 Don't connect 5 volts as an input to any of the GPIO pins as this might cause damage.

Now that you know the pins you have to connect to, you'll connect the sonar sensor. However, there is a problem, as you can't connect the 5-volt return from the sonar sensor directly to the Raspberry Pi GPIO pins; they want a maximum of 3.3 volts as input. You need to build a voltage divider that will reduce the 5 volts to 3.3 volts. This can be done with two resistors, which are connected as shown in the following diagram:

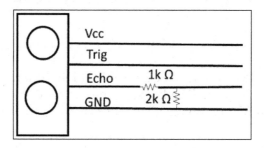

 For more information on how the voltage divider works in this configuration, refer to http://www.modmypi.com/blog/hc-sr04-ultrasonic-range-sensor-on-the-raspberry-pi.

The combination of these two resistors will reduce the voltage to the desired levels. Here is the circuit, as shown on the breadboard:

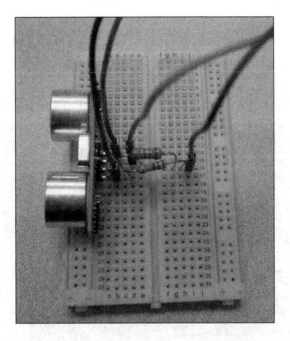

Finally, connect the sensor to the Raspberry Pi Zero, as shown:

Now that the device is connected, you'll need a bit of code to read in the value, make sure it is settled (it produces a stable measurement), and then convert it to distance.

Raspberry Pi Zero and the sonar sensor code

Here is Python code to communicate with the sonar sensor:

```
pi@raspberrypi: ~                                          _  □  X
File Edit Options Buffers Tools Python Help
#!/user/bin/python

import RPi.GPIO as io
import time

io.setmode(io.BCM)

trig = 23
echo = 24

io.setup(trig,io.OUT)
io.setup(echo,io.IN)

io.setup(trig, False)
time.sleep(1)
io.output(trig, True)
time.sleep(.00001)
io.output(trig, False)

while io.input(echo) == 0:
    start = time.time()

while io.input(echo) == 1:
    end = time.time()

duration = end - start
distance = duration * 17150
distance = round(distance, 2)
print "Distance: ", distance, " cm"
io.cleanup()

-UU-:----F1  sonar.py       All L1     (Python) -------------------------
For information about GNU Emacs and the GNU system, type C-h C-a.
```

Here is an explanation of the code:

- `#!/usr/bin/python`: This line lets you run this program without having to type python before the filename. You'll learn how to do this at the end of these instructions.

- `import RPi.GPIO as io`: This lets you import the `RPi` library, which will allow you to control the GPIO pins.

- `import time`: The `time` library provides several time-based functions. In this case, you'll use it to pause the program for a known amount of time and also measure a certain time delay.

- `io.setmode(io.BCM)`: This sets the specification mode of the GPIO pins to Broadcom SOC channel number (BCM). This means you will specify the GPIO numbers of the pins you want to control, instead of the actual physical pin values.

- `trig = 23`: This assigns the value 23 to the `trig` variable.

- `echo = 24`: This assigns the value 24 to the `echo` variable.

- `io.setup(trig, io.OUT)`: This sets the GPIO pin 23 to an output.

- `io.setup(echo, io.IN)`: This sets the GPIO pin 24 to an input.

- `io.setup(trig, False)`: This will output a zero to the trig line, pin 23.

- `time.sleep(1)`: This command will cause the program to pause for one second.

- `io.output(trig, True)`: This will output a one, 5 volts, to the trig line, pin 23.

- `time.sleep(.00001)`: This will cause the program to wait approximately 10 microseconds.

- `io.output(trig, False)`: This will output a zero to the trig line, pin 23.

- `while io.input(echo) == 0:`: While the input to pin 24 is zero.

- `    start = time.time()`: Reset the start time continuously. When pin 24 goes high, `start` will hold the latest time that the value of pin 24 was low.

- `while io.input(echo) == 1:`: Do the following set of commands while the input pin 24 is 1.

- `    end = time.time()`: Resets the end time continuously. When pin 24 goes low, `end` will hold the latest time that the value of pin 24 was high.

- `duration = end - start`: Duration will now hold the time distance between the end and start time.

- `distance = duration * 17150`: Distance converts the duration to a distance value.

- `distance = round(distance, 2)`: Round the distance to two decimal places.

- `print "Distance: ", distance, " cm"`: Print out the distance.

- `io.cleanup()`: Reset the interface.

Now you should save and run the program and get a result, as shown in the following screenshot:

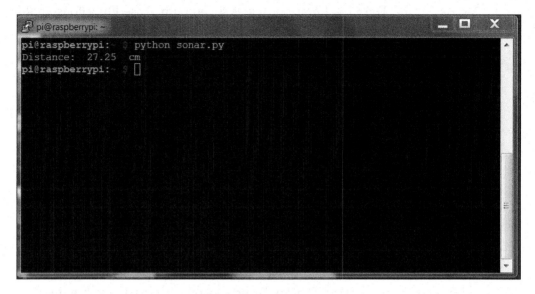

Now you can sense the distance with Raspberry Pi Zero!

Connecting a digital compass to Raspberry Pi Zero

Now you've created some pretty basic connections to Raspberry Pi Zero, turning lines on and off and sensing a high or low signal. Now let's explore one of the other interfaces available on Raspberry Pi Zero, the I2C interface. To do this, you'll connect a digital compass with this sort of interface.

>  For more on the I2C interface, see http://www.robot-electronics.co.uk/i2c-tutorial.

There are several chips that provide digital compass capability; one of the most common is the **HMC5883L**, a *3-axis* digital compass chip. This chip is packaged in a module by several companies but almost all of them result in a similar interface.

Here is an image of the **GY-271 HMC5883L**, a triple-axis compass magnetometer sensor module available with a number of online retailers:

This type of digital compass uses magnetic sensors to measure the earth's magnetic field. The output of these sensors is then made accessible to the outside world through a set of registers that allow the user to set things, such as the sample rate and continuous or single sampling. The *X*, *Y*, and *Z* directions are the output using registers as well.

This chip communicates with Raspberry Pi Zero using the **Inter IC (I2C)** bus. There are three serial busses available on Raspberry Pi's GPIO interfaces. The first is a standard **Universal Asynchronous Receiver/Transmitter (UART)** interface. The UART interface uses one pin for the RX, or receive signal, and one pin for the TX, or transmit signal. The UART takes bytes of data and transmits the individual bits in a sequential order. At the destination, a second UART reassembles the bits into bytes. This interface is limited to communicating with a single external device. For more information on the UART interface and how it works, go to `https://www.freebsd.org/doc/en/articles/serial-uart/`.

The second interface that is available is the I2C interface. The I2C interface is similar to the UART interface; it also communicates using two lines, in this case a data-line and a clock-line. However, it is a bit more complex, as it allows communication between one master and many slave devices. It does this by addressing the device the master device wants to communicate with. For more information on the I2C interface, see `http://www.robot-electronics.co.uk/i2c-tutorial`.

The final interface that is available is the **Serial Peripheral Interface (SPI)** interface. As with the I2C interface, the SPI interface allows for communication between a master device and more than one slave device. However, each slave is selected using a different select data line. SPI masters communicate with slaves using the **serial clock (SCK)**, **Master Out Slave In (MOSI)**, **Master In Slave Out (MISO)**, and **Slave Select (SS)** lines. The SCK, MOSI, and MISO signals can be shared by slaves, while each slave has a unique SS line. For more information on the SPI interface, see `http://www.corelis.com/education/SPI_Tutorial.htm`.

Since the device you are going to use is an I2C device, at the back of the compass module will be three connections, one for power (VCC), one for ground (GND), one for the clock (SCL), and one for data (SDA). The connections are labeled as shown in the following image:

To connect the device, you need to connect the I2C interface pins on Raspberry Pi Zero. Here is the detail of the GPIO pins:

I2C Interface			
	Pin 1 3.3V	☐ ○	Pin 2 5V
	Pin 3 GPIO2	○ ○	Pin 4 5V
	Pin 5 GPIO3	○ ○	Pin 6 GND
	Pin 7 GPIO4	○ ○	Pin 8 GPIO14
	Pin 9 GND	○ ○	Pin 10 GPIO15
	Pin 11 GPIO17	○ ○	Pin 12 GPIO18
	Pin 13 GPIO27	○ ○	Pin 14 GND
	Pin 15 GPIO22	○ ○	Pin 16 GPIO23
	Pin 17 3.3V	○ ○	Pin 18 GPIO24
	Pin 19 GPIO10	○ ○	Pin 20 GND
	Pin 21 GPIO9	○ ○	Pin 22 GPIO25
	Pin 23 GPIO11	○ ○	Pin 24 GPIO8
	Pin 25 GND	○ ○	Pin 26 GPIO7
	Pin 27 ID_SD	○ ○	Pin 28 ID_SC
	Pin 29 GPIO5	○ ○	Pin 30 GND
	Pin 31 GPIO6	○ ○	Pin 32 GPIO12
	Pin 33 GPIO13	○ ○	Pin 34 GND
	Pin 35 GPIO19	○ ○	Pin 36 GPIO16
	Pin 37 GPIO26	○ ○	Pin 38 GPIO20
	Pin 39 GND	○ ○	Pin 40 GPIO21

Serial Interface, SPI Interface, EEPROM

You'll connect the device to pins 1, 3, 5, 7, and 9. For these connections, you'll want female-to-female jumper wires:

1. Connect the VCC pin on the module to **Pin 1 3.3 V** on Raspberry Pi Zero and **GND** to **Pin 9 GND**.

2. Then connect **SCL** on the module to **Pin 5 GPIO3** and **SDA** to **Pin 3 GPIO2** on the Raspberry Pi Zero. Note that you will not connect the **Data Ready (DRDY)** pin on the compass; this is an optional connection for the device. Here are the connections:

Now, you are ready to communicate with the device.

Accessing the compass programmatically

Now that the device is connected, you'll need to configure access via the software. Here are the steps:

1. In order to access the compass capability, you'll need to enable the I2C library on Raspberry Pi Zero. To enable this bus, run `sudo raspi-config` and select **9 Advanced Options**, as follows:

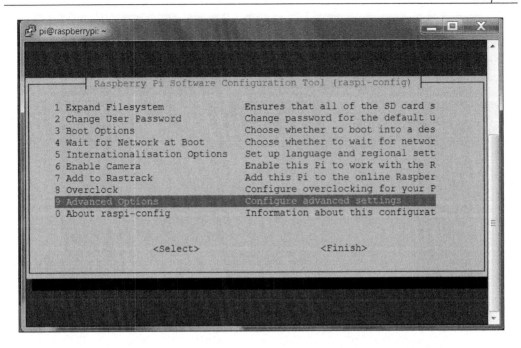

2. Then go to the **A7 I2C** selection and enable the I2C, as shown in the following screenshot:

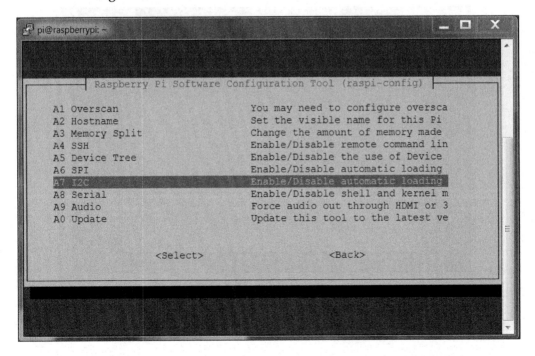

3. Select **Yes** to enable the I2C interface, as shown in the following screenshot:

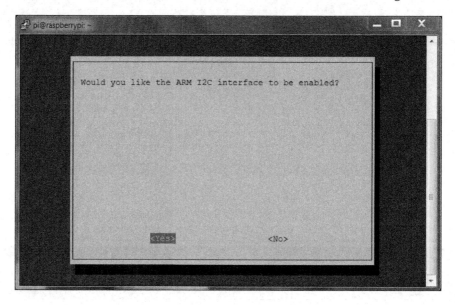

4. Select **OK** on the next screen, then **Yes** on the screen that asks whether you want the I2C kernel module loaded by default, as shown:

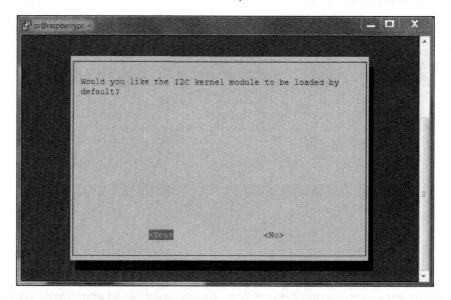

5. Select **OK** to return to the main selection, then exit and reboot your Raspberry Pi Zero.

Now you can sense whether the device is connected. Install the I2C toolkit by typing `sudo apt-get install i2c-tools`. You can see whether I2C is enabled by typing `sudo i2cdetect -y 1` and then you should see something similar to the following screenshot:

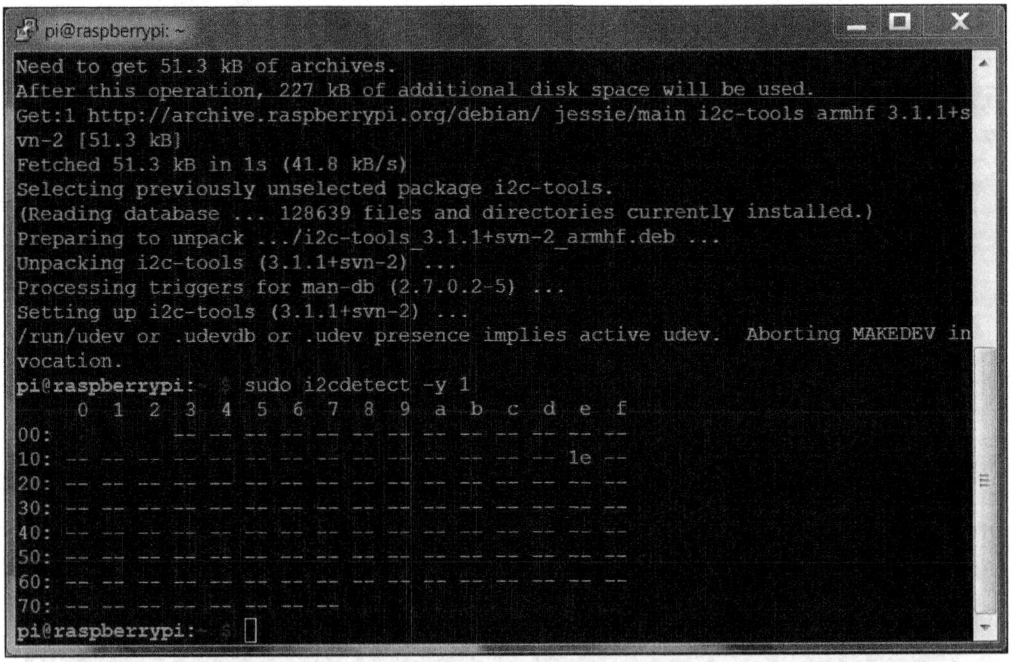

You can see the device at `1e`. Now you can communicate with your digital compass. Here are the steps:

1. You'll need to create a Python program. Before you create your Python code, you need to install the **SMBus** capability to access I2C. This can be done by typing `sudo apt-get install python-smbus`.

2. Now reboot Raspberry Pi; you can use the smbus library ability to read and write from your I2C device. Fortunately, in this case the device comes with some example code on how to configure the device and then read a value's. Here is an example of a Python code:

```
pi@raspberrypi: ~
File Edit Options Buffers Tools Python Help
#!/usr/bin/python
import smbus
import time
import math
bus = smbus.SMBus(1)
address = 0x1e

def read_byte(adr):
    return bus.read_byte_data(address, adr)
def read_word(adr):
    high = bus.read_byte_data(address, adr)
    low = bus.read_byte_data(address, adr+1)
    val = (high << 8) + low
    return val
def read_word_2c(adr):
    val = read_word(adr)
    if (val >= 0x8000):
        return -((65535 - val) + 1)
    else:
        return val
def write_byte(adr, value):
    bus.write_byte_data(address, adr, value)

write_byte(0, 0b01110000) # Set to 8 samples @ 15Hz
write_byte(1, 0b00100000) # 1.3 gain LSb / Gauss 1090 (default)
write_byte(2, 0b00000000) # Continuous sampling
scale = 0.92
x_out = read_word_2c(3) * scale
y_out = read_word_2c(7) * scale
z_out = read_word_2c(5) * scale
bearing  = math.atan2(y_out, x_out)
if (bearing < 0):
    bearing += 2 * math.pi
print "Bearing: ", math.degrees(bearing)

-UU-:----F1  compass.py      All L14     (Python) ----------------------------
```

Run the code by typing `python compass.py` and you should see the following output:

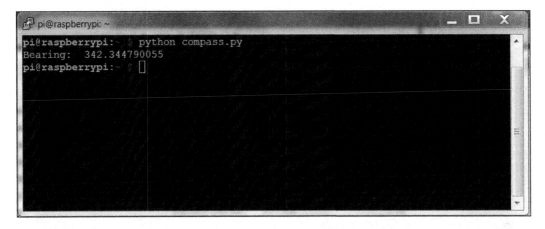

As you move the device around, you should see this value change to reflect the device's compass direction.

This is just an example of how to connect an I2C device. There are a number of different other devices that can be connected to the GPIO bus of Raspberry Pi Zero.

Summary

That's it! You've completed your very first hardware project. You should now feel at least a little comfortable with Raspberry Pi Zero's GPIO bus. In the next chapter, you'll learn how to create a Raspberry Pi Zero controlled car.

4

Building and Controlling a Simple Wheeled Robot

You should now be familiar with how to program your Raspberry Pi Zero and how to communicate with the outside world with the GPIO. Now, let's actually build a mobile project. Perhaps the easiest way to make your projects mobile is to use a wheeled platform. In this chapter, you will be introduced to some of the basics of manipulating DC motors and using the Raspberry Pi Zero to control the speed and direction of your wheeled platform.

In this chapter, you will learn how to perform the following actions:

- Using the Raspberry Pi Zero GPIO to control a DC motor
- Controlling your mobile platform programmatically using the Raspberry Pi Zero
- Implementing some simple path planning algorithms on the Raspberry Pi Zero

The basic platform

You'll need to add some hardware, specifically a wheeled or tracked platform, to make your project mobile. You're going to use a platform that uses differential motion to propel and steer the vehicle. This simply means that, instead of turning the wheels, you're going to vary the speed and direction of the two motors that drive the wheels or tracks. There are a lot of choices. Some come fully assembled while others require some assembly; alternatively you can buy the components and build your own custom mobile platform.

Let's look at a couple of the more popular units that come fully assembled or can be assembled with simple tools (a screwdriver or pliers). The simplest mobile platform is one that has two DC motors, with each motor controlling a single wheel. On the wheeled platform, there is a small wheel or ball in the front or at the back. Here is one example of a wheeled platform, available at many online electronics retailers:

Here is another simple wheeled platform, also sold by many online electronics retailers:

This one also needs to be assembled but it is fairly straightforward. You could also choose a tracked platform instead of a wheeled platform. A tracked platform has more traction but is not as nimble, as it takes a longer distance to turn. Again, manufacturers make pre-assembled units. The following image is an example of a pre-assembled tracked platform made by Dagu. It's called the Dagu Rover 5 Tracked Chassis:

As part of the platform, you'll need a mobile power supply for the Raspberry Pi Zero and your vehicle. I personally like the external 5V rechargeable cell phone batteries which are available at almost any place that sells cell phones. These batteries can be charged using a USB cable connected either through a DC power supply or directly from a computer USB port, as shown in the following image:

You'll also need a USB cable to connect your battery to the Raspberry Pi Zero. Now that you have the basic platform, you're ready to start controlling it with the Raspberry Pi Zero.

There are two choices here and I'll walk you through both. Firstly, you can use a chip called an H-bridge, plug it into your electronic breadboard, and control the DC motors with connections to the GPIO of the Raspberry Pi Zero. The second choice is to use a dedicated motor controller board designed to connect directly onto the Raspberry Pi Zero's GPIO pins. Let's cover the H-bridge option first.

Controlling an H-bridge interface to the DC motors

The first step to make the platform mobile is to connect the Raspberry Pi Zero to your H-bridge. This allows you to control the speed of each wheel (or track) independently. Before you get started, let's spend some time learning the basics of motor control. Whether you choose the two-wheeled mobile platform or the tracked platform, the basic movement control is the same. The unit moves by engaging the motors. If the desired direction is straight ahead, the motors are run at the same speed. If you want to turn the unit, the motors are run at different speeds. The unit can turn in a circle if you run one motor forwards and the other one backwards.

The DC motors are fairly straightforward devices. The speed and direction of the motor is controlled by the magnitude and polarity of the voltage applied to its terminals. The higher the voltage, the faster the motor will turn. If you reverse the polarity of the voltage, you can reverse the direction in which the motor turns.

The magnitude and polarity of the voltage are not the only important factors when you think about controlling the motors. The power that your motor can apply to move your platform is also determined by the voltage and the current supplied to its terminals.

There are GPIO (short for general purpose input-output) pins on the Raspberry Pi Zero that you can use to control the voltage and drive your motors. These GPIO pins provide direct access to some of the control lines available from the processor itself. However, the unit cannot obtain enough current and your motors will not be able to generate enough power to move your mobile platform. This can also cause physical damage to your Raspberry Pi Zero board.

You can, however, connect your Raspberry Pi Zero to the DC motors by using an H-bridge DC motor controller. An H-bridge is a fairly simple device. It basically consists of a set of electronic switches and provides the additional functionality of allowing the direction of the current to be reversed so that the motor can be run in either forward or reverse directions.

Let's start this example by building the H-bridge circuit and controlling just one motor. To do this, you need to get an H-bridge. One of the most common options is the L293 dual H-bridge chip. This chip allows you to control the direction of the DC motors. These are available at most electronics stores and online. Once you have your H-bridge, build the circuit as shown in the following image with the Raspberry Pi Zero, the motor, the jumper wires, a 4AA battery holder, and a breadboard:

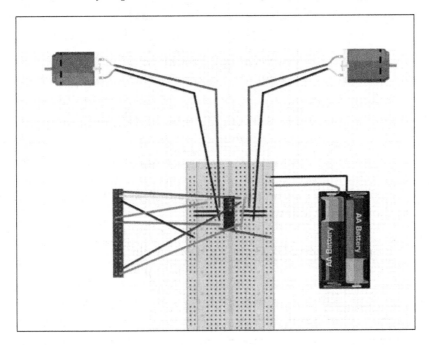

Also, before you start connecting wires, here is an image of the GPIO pins on the Raspberry Pi Zero board:

```
Pin 1 3.3V      □ ○   Pin 2 5V
Pin 3 GPIO2     ○ ○   Pin 4 5V
Pin 5 GPIO3     ○ ○   Pin 6 GND
Pin 7 GPIO4     ○ ○   Pin 8 GPIO14
Pin 9 GND       ○ ○   Pin 10 GPIO15
Pin 11 GPIO17   ○ ○   Pin 12 GPIO18
Pin 13 GPIO27   ○ ○   Pin 14 GND
Pin 15 GPIO22   ○ ○   Pin 16 GPIO23
Pin 17 3.3V     ○ ○   Pin 18 GPIO24
Pin 19 GPIO10   ○ ○   Pin 20 GND
Pin 21 GPIO9    ○ ○   Pin 22 GPIO25
Pin 23 GPIO11   ○ ○   Pin 24 GPIO8
Pin 25 GND      ○ ○   Pin 26 GPIO7
Pin 27 ID_SD    ○ ○   Pin 28 ID_SC
Pin 29 GPIO5    ○ ○   Pin 30 GND
Pin 31 GPIO6    ○ ○   Pin 32 GPIO12
Pin 33 GPIO13   ○ ○   Pin 34 GND
Pin 35 GPIO19   ○ ○   Pin 36 GPIO16
Pin 37 GPIO26   ○ ○   Pin 38 GPIO20
Pin 39 GND      ○ ○   Pin 40 GPIO21
```

You need to connect these pins on the Raspberry Pi Zero GPIO to the pins on the H-bridge, as shown in the following table:

Raspberry Pi Zero GPIO pin	H-bridge pin
4 (5V)	1 (Enable pin)
13 (GPIO 27)	2 (Forward)
15 (GPIO 22)	7 (Backward)
4 (5V)	11 (Enable 2)
38 (GPIO 6)	10 (Forward)
40 (GPIO 13)	15 (Backward)
6 (GND)	4, 5, 12, 13 (GND)
2 (5 Volts)	16 (VCC)
Battery positive terminal	8 (Vc)
Battery negative terminal	GND (connect to the same GND as previous GND pins)

Once you have the connections, you can test the system. To make this all work, you need to add some code, which we will see in the next section.

Controlling your mobile platform programmatically using the Raspberry Pi Zero

Now that you have your basic motor controller functionality up and running, you need to connect both motor controllers to the Raspberry Pi Zero. This section will cover this and also show you how to control your entire platform programmatically.

You are going to use Python in your initial attempts to control the motor. It is very straightforward to code, run, and debug your code in Python. The first Python program you are going to create is shown in the following screenshot:

```
#!/usr/bin/python
import RPi.GPIO as io

io.setmode(io.BCM)
in1_pin1 = 27
in2_pin1 = 22
in1_pin2 = 20
in2_pin2 = 21

io.setup(in1_pin1, io.OUT)
io.setup(in2_pin1, io.OUT)
io.setup(in1_pin2, io.OUT)
io.setup(in2_pin2, io.OUT)

def forward():
    io.output(in1_pin1, True)
    io.output(in2_pin1, False)
    io.output(in1_pin2, True)
    io.output(in2_pin2, False)

def reverse():
    io.output(in1_pin1, False)
    io.output(in2_pin1, True)
    io.output(in1_pin2, False)
    io.output(in2_pin2, True)

def stop():
    io.output(in1_pin1, False)
    io.output(in2_pin1, False)
    io.output(in1_pin2, False)
    io.output(in2_pin2, False)

while True:
    cmd = raw_input("Enter f (forward) or r (reverse) or s (stop): ")
    direction = cmd[0]
    if direction == "f":
        forward()
    if direction == "r":
        reverse()
    if direction == "s":
        stop()
```

Perform the following steps to create this program:

To create this program, create a directory called dcmotor in your home directory by typing `mkdir dcmotor` and then type `cd dcmotor`. Now, open the file by typing `emacs dcmotor.py` (if you are using a different editor, open a new file with the `dcmotor.py` name).

Now, enter the program. Let's go through the program step by step:

- `#!/usr/bin/python`: This line lets you run the program without having to type `python` before the filename. You'll learn how to do this at the end of these instructions.

- `import RPi.GPIO as io`: This lets you import the RPi library, which allows you to control the GPIO pins.

- `io.setmode(io.BCM)`: This sets the specification mode of the GPIO pins to **Broadcom SOC channel (BCM)** number. This means that you will specify the GPIO numbers of the pins you want to control instead of the actual physical pin values.

- `in1_pin1 = 27`: This assigns the value 27 to the in1_pin1 variable.

- `in2_pin1 = 22`: This assigns the value 22 to the in1_pin1 variable.

- `in1_pin2 = 20`: This assigns the value 20 to the in1_pin1 variable.

- `in2_pin2 = 21`: This assigns the value 21 to the in1_pin1 variable.

- `io.setup(in1_pin1, io.OUT)`: This sets GPIO pin 27 to an output control.

- `io.setup(in2_pin1, io.OUT)`: This sets GPIO pin 22 to an output control.

- `io.setup(in1_pin2, io.OUT)`: This sets GPIO pin 20 to an output control.

- `io.setup(in2_pin2, io.OUT)`: This sets GPIO pin 21 to an output control.

- `def forward()`:: This defines the forward function. You have to turn on GPIO 27 and GPIO 20 and turn off GPIO 22 and GPIO 21.

- `io.output(in1_pin1, True)`: Output a 3.3 volt signal on in1_pin1 (this is GPIO 27).

- `io.output(in2_pin1, False)`: Output 0 volts on in2_pin1 (this is GPIO 22).

- `io.output(in1_pin2, True)`: Output a high voltage on in1_pin2 (this is GPIO 20).

- `io.output(in2_pin2, False)`: Output 0 volts on `in2_pin2` (this is GPIO 21).
- `def reverse()::` This defines the reverse function. You'll turn on GPIO 22 and GPIO 21, and turn off GPIO 27 and GPIO 20.
- `io.output(in1_pin1, False)`: Output 0 volts on `in1_pin1` (this is GPIO 27).
- `io.output(in2_pin1, True)`: Output a high voltage on `in2_pin1` (this is GPIO 22).
- `io.output(in1_pin2, False)`: Output 0 volts on `in1_pin2` (this is GPIO 20).
- `io.output(in2_pin2, True)`: Output a high voltage on `in2_pin2` (this is GPIO 21).
- `def stop()::` This defines the stop function. You set the level to 0 on the pins off GPIO 22, GPIO 21, GPIO 27, and GPIO 20.
- `io.output(in1_pin1, False)`: Output 0 volts on `in1_pin1` (this is GPIO 27).
- `io.output(in2_pin1, False)`: Output 0 volts on `in2_pin1` (this is GPIO 22).
- `io.output(in1_pin2, False)`: Output 0 volts on `in1_pin2` (this is GPIO 20).
- `io.output(in2_pin2, False)`: Output 0 volts on `in2_pin2` (this is GPIO 21).
- `while True::` This performs loops over and over. You can stop the program by pressing *Ctrl + C*.
- `cmd = raw_input("Enter f (forward) or r (reverse) or s (stop): ")`: Enter a character for what you want the robot to do.
- `direction = cmd[0]`: Take only the first character of the input.
- `if direction == "f"::` If the direction is `"f"`, then execute the next statement.
- `forward()`: Execute the forward function.
- `if direction == "r"::` If the direction is `"f"`, then execute the next statement.
- `reverse()`: Execute the reverse function.
- `if direction == "s"::` If the direction is `"f"`, then execute the next statement.
- `stop()`: Execute the stop function.

You can now run your program. In order to do this, type
`sudo python ./dcmotor.py`. When you enter `f`, the motors should
run forward; with `r` they should run backward; and with `s`, they should
stop. You can now control the motor with Python. Additionally, you may
want to make this program available to run from the command line. Type
`chmod +x dcmotor.py`. If you now type `ls` (list programs), you'll see that
your program is now green, which means that you can execute it directly.
Now you can type `sudo ./dcmotor.py` and the program will run.

Now that you know the basics of commanding your mobile platform, feel free to add
even more functions and commands to make your mobile platform move in different
ways. Running just one motor will make the platform turn, as will running both
motors in opposite directions.

Controlling the speed of your motors with PWM

The previous example either turned the motors on to full speed or turned them off.
You may want to configure your motors to run at different speeds. This can be done
by using **Pulse Width Modulation (PWM)** to adjust the speed. PWM simply defines
a way of changing the voltage of the signal by sending a series of pulses of equal
value and changing the width of each pulse. The wider the pulse, the higher the
average voltage delivered to the receiver. The DC motors that you are using
respond to this higher average voltage by spinning faster.

The Raspberry Pi Zero GPIO can create PWM signals. The code snippet to do this is
shown in the following screenshot:

```
pi@raspberrypi: ~/dcmotor
File Edit Options Buffers Tools Python Help
#!/usr/bin/python
import RPi.GPIO as io

io.setmode(io.BCM)
in1_pin1 = 27
in2_pin1 = 22
in1_pin2 = 20
in2_pin2 = 21

io.setup(in1_pin1, io.OUT)
p1 = io.PWM(in1_pin1, 50)
p1.start(0)
io.setup(in2_pin1, io.OUT)
p2 = io.PWM(in2_pin1, 50)
p2.start(0)
io.setup(in1_pin2, io.OUT)
p3 = io.PWM(in1_pin2, 50)
p3.start(0)
io.setup(in2_pin2, io.OUT)
p4 = io.PWM(in2_pin2, 50)
p4.start(0)

def forward():
    p1.start(50)
    p2.start(0)
    p3.start(50)
    p4.start(0)

def reverse():
    p1.start(0)
    p2.start(50)
    p3.start(0)
    p4.start(50)

def stop():
    p1.start(0)
    p2.start(0)
    p3.start(0)
    p4.start(0)

while True:
-UU-:----F1   dcmotor.py      Top L1      (Python)---------------------------
```

The following is an explanation of the lines of code that you just added:

- `io.setup(in2_pin1, io.OUT)`: This sets GPIO 27 to an output.

- `p1 = io.PWM(in1_pin1, 50)`: Instead of just on or off settings, this PWM setting allows the programmer to set the relative width of the pulse. This initializes this functionality on GPIO 27.

- `p1.start(0)`: This starts the pulses on `p1`, GPIO 27, with a pulse width of 0 percent, or off.

- `io.setup(in2_pin1, io.OUT)`: This sets GPIO 22 to an output.

- `p2 = io.PWM(in2_pin1, 50)`: This initializes this functionality on GPIO 22.
- `p2.start(0)`: This starts the pulses on `p2`, GPIO 22, with a pulse width of 0 percent, or off.
- `io.setup(in1_pin2, io.OUT)`: This sets GPIO 20 to an output.
- `p3 = io.PWM(in1_pin2, 50)`: This initializes this functionality on GPIO 20.
- `p3.start(0)`: This starts the pulses on `p3`, GPIO 20, with a pulse width of 0 percent, or off.
- `io.setup(in2_pin2, io.OUT)`: This sets GPIO 21 to an output.
- `p4 = io.PWM(in2_pin2, 50)`: This initializes this functionality on GPIO 21.
- `p4.start(0)`: This starts the pulses on `p3`, GPIO 21, with a pulse width of 0 percent, or off.
- `def forward(50):`: This function moves the unit forward by setting the pulse width in a forward direction to 50 percent.
- `p1.start(50)`: This sets the value of `p1` (GPIO 27) to 50 percent on and 50 percent off. This should result in the motor running forward at half speed.
- `p2.start(0)`: This sets the value of `p2` (GPIO 22) to 0 percent. This effectively turns this pin off.
- `p3.start(50)`: This sets the value of `p3` (GPIO 20) to 50 percent on and 50 percent off. This should result in the motor running forward at half speed.
- `p4.start(0)`: This sets the value of `p4` (GPIO21) to 0 percent. This effectively turns this pin off.
- `def reverse(50):`: This function moves the unit in reverse by setting the pulse width in the reverse direction to 50 percent.
- `p1.start(0)`: This sets the value of `p1` (GPIO 27) to 0 percent. This effectively turns this pin off.
- `p2.start(50)`: This sets the value of `p2` (GPIO 22) to 50 percent on and 50 percent off. This should result in the motor running in reverse at half speed.
- `p3.start(0)`: This sets the value of `p3` (GPIO 20) to 0 percent. This effectively turns this pin off.
- `p4.start(50)`: This sets the value of `p4` (GPIO21) to 50 percent on and 50 percent off. This should result in the motor running in reverse at half speed.
- `def stop():`: This function sets all PWM signals to 0 percent, effectively stopping the motors.
- `p1.start(0)`: This sets the value of `p1` (GPIO 27) to 0 percent. This effectively turns this pin off.

- `p2.start(0)`: This sets the value of p2 (GPIO 22) to 0 percent. This effectively turns this pin off.

- `p3.start(0)`: This sets the value of p3 (GPIO 20) to 0 percent. This effectively turns this pin off.

- `p4.start(0)`: This sets the value of p4 (GPIO 21) to 0 percent. This effectively turns this pin off.

The rest of the program is the same as the first `dcmotor.py` file. Running this program should result in the unit running at half the speed of the first program. You can easily change this speed by changing the value sent to the various start functions.

You can also control the DC motors by using a DC motor controller to connect to the Raspberry Pi Zero directly. For example, Pololu, who can be found at `https://www.pololu.com/`, make the DRV8835 Dual Motor Driver Kit for the Raspberry Pi. Another option is the RasPiRobot Board V2 available at `http://www.monkmakes.com/`. For this example, we will use the RasPiRobot Board V2.

Using a motor controller board to control the DC motors

To build this project, you'll start by installing the motor controller board on top of the Raspberry Pi Zero, like this:

The board provides the drive signals for the DC motors on the vehicle. You can also turn the vehicle by driving each motor separately. You can change the vehicle's direction and make very sharp turns by reversing the signals. The following steps show how to connect the motor control board:

1. Connect the battery power connector to the power connector on the board. Use a 6 to 7.4 volts battery; you can either use a 4 AA battery holder or a 2S LiPo RC battery. Connect the ground and power wires to the motor control board as shown:

2. Next, connect one of the drive signals to the motor 1 connector on the board. Connect motor 1 to the right motor and motor 2 to the left, as shown:

3. Then, connect the second drive connector to the motor 2 connector on the board. The entire set of connections should look like this:

Now you are ready to drive your vehicle using the Raspberry Pi Zero.

Controlling the vehicle using the Raspberry Pi Zero in Python

The first step to take advantage of the functionality is to install the library associated with the control board, which can be found at http://www.monkmakes.com/?page_id=698. You need to connect your Raspberry Pi Zero to the Internet with either a wired or WLAN connection. Issue the following commands in a terminal window on your Raspberry Pi Zero:

1. Type wget https://github.com/simonmonk/raspirobotboard2/raw/master/python/dist/rrb2-1.1.tar.gz: This will download the library to your Raspberry Pi.

2. Type `tar -xzf rrb2-1.1.tar.gz`: This unarchives the library.

3. Type `cd rrb2-1.1`: This changes directory to the location of the files.

4. Type `sudo python setup.py install`: This installs the libraries.

Now that you have the library code installed, you need to create some Python code that will allow you to access the two motors. The first part of the code should look as follows:

```python
import RPi.GPIO as GPIO
import time
from rrb2 import *
import tty
import sys
import termios
def getch():
    fd = sys.stdin.fileno()
    old_settings = termios.tcgetattr(fd)
    tty.setraw(sys.stdin.fileno())
    ch = sys.stdin.read(1)
    termios.tcsetattr(fd, termios.TCSADRAIN, old_settings)
    return ch
pwmPin = 18
dc = 10
GPIO.setmode(GPIO.BCM)
GPIO.setup(pwmPin, GPIO.OUT)
pwm = GPIO.PWM(pwmPin, 320)
rr = RRB2()
pwm.start(dc)
rr.set_led1(1)
var = 'n'
speed1 = 0
speed2 = 0
direction1 = 1
direction2 = 1

while var != 'q':
    var = getch()
    if var == 'l':
```

-UU-:**--F1   xmodControl.py   Top L1   (Python)---------------------------

The second part of the code that drives the two different motors, based on whether you want to go forwards, backwards, or turn right or left, is as follows:

```
pi@raspberrypi: ~/tracked
File Edit Options Buffers Tools Python Help
while var != 'q':
    var = getch()
    if var == 'l':
        speed1 = 1
        direction1 = 1
        speed2 = 1
        direction2 = 0
        stop = 1
    if var == 'r':
        speed1 = 1
        direction1 = 0
        speed2 = 1
        direction2 = 1
        stop = 1
    if var == 'f':
        speed1 = 1
        direction1 = 1
        speed2 = 1
        direction2 = 1
        stop = 0
    if var == 'b':
        speed1 = 1
        direction1 = 0
        speed2 = 1
        direction2 = 0
        stop = 0
    if var == 's':
        speed1 = 0
        direction1 = 0
        speed2 = 0
        direction2 = 0
    rr.set_motors(speed1, direction1, speed2, direction2)
    if stop == 1:
        time.sleep(1)
        rr.set_motors(0, 0, 0, 0)
GPIO.cleanup()

-UU-:----F1   track.py        Bot L40    (Python)--------------------------------
```

The `rr.set_motors()` function allows you to specify the speed and direction of each motor independently. This program takes in a single character and then sends a command to the motors. `f` moves the vehicle forward, `b` moves it backward, `l` turns it left, `r` turns it right, and `s` stops the vehicle.

Now that you have the basic code to drive your tracked vehicle, you can modify it so that each action is contained in a function. In that way, you can call these functions from another Python program. You also need to add calibrated movement so that your tracked vehicle is able to turn at a certain angle and move forwards a set distance. The following example is what the code should look like:

```python
import RPi.GPIO as GPIO
import time
from rrb2 import *

rr = RRB2()

def init_vehicle():
    rr.set_led1(1)

def turn_left(angle):
    rr.set_motors(1, 1, 1, 0)
    time.sleep(angle/20)
    rr.set_motors(0, 0, 0, 0)

def turn_right(angle):
    rr.set_motors(1, 0, 1, 1)
    time.sleep(angle/20)
    rr.set_motors(0, 0, 0, 0)

def forward(value):
    rr.set_motors(1, 1, 1, 1)
    time.sleep(value)
    rr.set_motors(0, 0, 0, 0)

def backward(value):
    rr.set_motors(1, 0, 1, 0)
    time.sleep(value)
    rr.set_motors(0, 0, 0, 0)

def stop():
    rr.set_motors(0, 0, 0, 0)

def cleanup():
    GPIO.cleanup()
```

```
-UU-:----F1    track.py        All L1      (Python)---------------------
```

The `time.sleep(angle/20)` command in the `turn_right(angle)` and `turn_left(angle)` functions allows the tracked vehicle to move for the right amount of time so that the vehicle moves through the desired angle. You may need to modify this number to get the correct angle of movement. The `time.sleep(value)` command moves the robot for a specific amount of time, based on the number given in the value.

If you have chosen to use the RasPiRobot Board V2 you can also use its special connections and libraries to connect the HC-SR04 sonar sensor. Here is a picture of the special connector on the board:

To use this connector, simply connect the VCC to the 5V, the Trig to the T connection, the Echo to the E connector, and the GND to the GND connection. You can then use the library for the motor controller board and simply call the function `rr.get_distance()`. Similarly, there is also a special connector and libraries for the I2C interface, if you want to add the compass to your mobile project.

Planning your path

Now that you have a wheeled or tracked vehicle, you may want to do some basic path planning. To do this, you need a framework to understand where your robot is and determine the location of the goal. One of the most common frameworks is an x-y grid. The following diagram is an example of this type of grid:

						Goal Point 6, 4
			Robot 3, 1			
Reference Point 0, 0						

There are three key points on this grid that you need to understand. Here is an explanation of them:

- The lower left point is a fixed reference position. The directions x and y are also fixed and all other positions are measured in relation to this position and these directions. Each unit is measured with regards to how far the unit travels in time in a single unit.

- Another important point is the starting location of your robot. Your robot will then keep track of its location using its x and y coordinates, the position with respect to some fixed reference position in the x direction, or the position with respect to some fixed reference position in the y direction to the goal. It uses the compass to keep track of these directions.

- The third important point is the position of the goal, also given in the x and y coordinates with respect to the fixed reference position. If you know the starting location and angle of your robot, you can plan an optimum (the shortest distance) path to this goal. To do this, you can use the goal location, the robot location and some fairly simple math to calculate the distance and angle from the robot to the goal.

To calculate the distance, use the following equation:

$$d = \sqrt{\left(\left(Xgoal - Xgoal\right)^2 + \left(Ygoal - Yrobot\right)^2\right)}$$

You use this equation to tell your robot how far to travel to reach the goal. A second equation tells your robot the angle at which it needs to travel:

$$\theta = \arctan \frac{\left(Ygoal - Yrobot\right)}{\left(Xgoal - Xrobot\right)}$$

[If you'd like a tutorial on the basic math of path planning, see
`https://www.khanacademy.org/math/trigonometry/`
`trigonometry-right-triangles`.]

Here is the graphical representation of these two pieces of information:

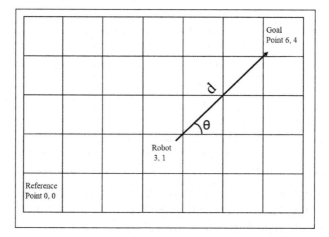

Now that you have a goal angle and distance, you can program your robot to move. To do this, you need to write a program to do the path planning and call the movement functions that you created earlier in the chapter. You need to know the distance that your robot will travel in a certain period of time so that you can tell your robot in time units, rather than distance units, how far to travel.

You also need to be able to translate the distance that might be covered by your robot in each time unit that you run the motor. If you know the angle and distance, you can move your robot towards the goal by turning the robot and then running it forward for a certain time.

Here are the steps that you need to follow:

1. Calculate the distance in units that your robot will travel to reach its goal. Convert this into a number of time units to realize this distance.

2. Calculate the angle at which your robot will need to travel to reach its goal. You need to use the compass and your robot's turn functions to turn and achieve this angle.

3. Now, call the `step` function a specified number of times to move your robot in the correct distance.

That's it. Now you can use some very simple Python code to execute these steps using the functions to move the robot forwards and turn it. In this case, it makes sense to create a file called `robotLib.py` with all the functions that do the actual servo settings to move the wheeled robot forwards and turn the robot. You then import these functions using the `from robotLib import *` statement so that your Python program can call these functions. This makes the path planning Python program much smaller and more manageable.

For more information on how to import functions from one Python file to another, refer to `http://www.tutorialspoint.com/python/python_modules.htm`.

Here is a screenshot of the program:

```python
#!/usr/bin/python
import time
from track import *
import math

xpos_robot = int(raw_input("Robot X Position: "))
ypos_robot = int(raw_input("Robot Y Position: "))
xpos_goal = int(raw_input("Goal X Position: "))
ypos_goal = int(raw_input("Goal Y Position: "))

distance = math.sqrt((xpos_goal - ypos_robot)**2 + (ypos_goal - ypos_robot)**2)
angle = round(math.degrees(math.atan2((ypos_goal - ypos_robot), (xpos_goal - xpos_robot))))
if angle < 0:
    angle = angle + 360
print (angle)
# Turn to the right bearing
if (angle) < 180:
    turn_right(angle)
else:
    turn_left(angle)
print (distance)
forward(distance)
```

In this program, the user determines the goal location and the robot decides on the shortest direction to the desired location by reading the angle. To make it simple, the robot is positioned in the grid, heading in the direction of an angle of 0 degrees. If the goal angle were less than 180 degrees, the robot would turn right. If it were greater than 180 degrees, the robot would turn left. The robot turns until the desired angle and the measured angle are within a few degrees of each other. Then, the robot takes the number of steps to reach the goal. As an additional challenge, you could add a loop to measure the actual angle and stop it when it reaches the target angle.

Summary

This chapter provided you with an opportunity to create a mobile platform for your Raspberry Pi Zero. You can add the sonar sensor or the compass from *Chapter 3, Accessing the GPIO Pins on Raspberry Pi Zero* to give it even more functionality. In the next chapter, you'll learn how to build a Raspberry Pi Zero platform robot with legs, an even more flexible mobile platform.

5
Building a Robot That Can Walk

Now that you are familiar with robots that can navigate using tracks or wheels, let's build one that can walk. Walking robots are interesting as they can navigate the terrain where wheeled or tracked vehicles can't go. They also provide advanced functions where the robot can use their legs for purposes other than walking.

In this chapter, you will build the basic quadruped platform. To do this you will learn:

- How servos work
- How to use the Raspberry Pi to control lots of servos using a servo controller
- Creating complex movements out of simple servo commands

Robots that can walk

In this chapter, you'll build a quadruped robots. You'll be using 12 servos so that each leg has three points that can move, or three **Degrees of Freedom (DOF)**. In this project, you'll control 12 servos at the same time; so it makes sense to use an external servo controller that can supply the control signals and supply voltages for all 12 servos. Since servos are the main component of this project, it will perhaps be useful to go through a tutorial on servos and learn how to control them.

How servo motors work

Servo motors are similar to DC motors; however, there is an important difference. While DC motors are generally designed to move in a continuous way—rotating 360 degrees at a given speed—servos are generally designed to move in a limited set of angles. In other words, in the DC motor world, you generally want your motors to spin with a continuous rotation speed that you control. In the servo world, you want your motor to move to a specific position that you control. This is done by sending a **Pulse-Width-Modulated (PWM)** signal on the control connector of the servo. PWM simply means that you are going to change the length of each pulse of electrical energy in order to control something. In this case, the length of this pulse will control the angle of the servo, as shown:

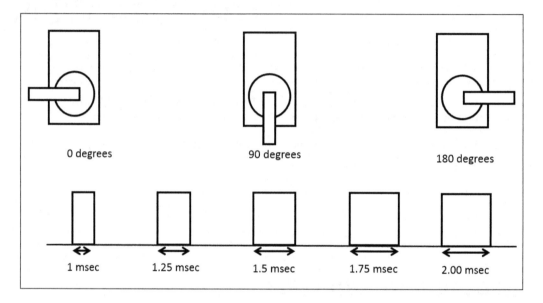

These pulses are sent out with a repetition rate of 60 Hz. You can position the servo at any angle by setting the correct control pulse.

Building the quadruped platform

You'll first need some parts, so you can build your quadruped robot. There are several kit possibilities out there, including at `http://www.trossenrobotics.com/p/PhantomX-AX-12-Quadruped.aspx`. However, such kits can be expensive; so for this example, you'll create your own kit using a set of **Lynxmotion** parts. These are available with several on-line retailers, such as `http://www.robotshop.com/`. To build this quadruped, you'll need two sets each of the two leg parts and then one set each of a body. Here are the parts with their Robotshop part number:

Quantity	Description
1	Lynxmotion Symmetric Quadrapod Body Kit - Mini QBK-02
2	Lynxmotion 3" Aluminum Femur Pair
2	Lynxmotion Robot Leg "A" Pair (No Servo) RL-01
4	Lynxmotion Aluminum Multipurpose Servo Bracket Two Pack ASB-04
2	Ball Bearing with Flange - 3mm ID (pair) Product Code: RB-Lyn-317

The last part is not a Lynxmotion part but a bearing that you'll need to connect the legs to the body.

You'll also need 12 standard-size servos. There are several possible choices, but I personally like the **Hitec** servos. They are very inexpensive servos that you can get at most hobby shops and on-line electronics retailers. Now its time to get to know some details about the selection of the model of servo. Servos come in different model numbers, primarily based on the amount of torque they can generate.

Torque is the force that the servo can exert to move the part connected to it. In this case, your servos will need to lift and move the weight associated with your quadruped, so you'll need a servo with enough torque to do this. In this case, I suggest you use eight model HS-485HB servos. You'll use these for the servos attached to the end of the leg and for the body. Then you'll use four model HS-645MG servos for the middle of the leg; this is the servo that will require the highest amount of torque. You can also just use twelve HS-645MG servos, but they are more expensive than the HS-485, so using the two different servos will be less expensive.

The following are the steps to assemble the quadruped:

1. Put the lower part of the right leg together; it should look like the following image:

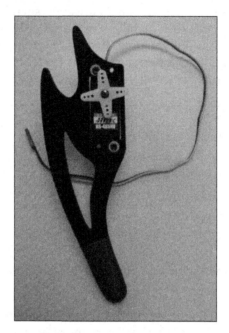

2. Now connect this assembly to an interconnecting piece, as shown:

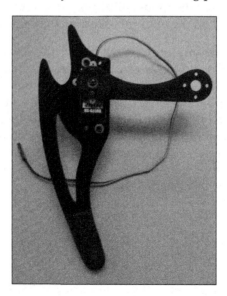

3. Complete the leg by connecting two of the servo brackets together at right angles, mounting the HS-645MG onto one of the brackets, and then connecting this servo to the interconnecting piece, as shown:

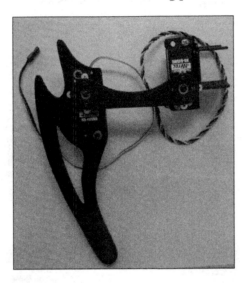

4. Put the other right leg together.

5. Now put the two left legs together by following the preceding steps, but in left leg configuration. They look similar to the following image:

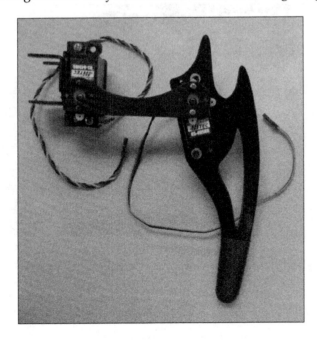

6. The next step is to build the body kit. You can find the instructions at `http://www.lynxmotion.com/images/html/sq3u-assembly.htm`.

7. Now connect each leg to the body kit. Here is a picture of the body kit:

8. Now, connect the servo to the empty servo bracket and the body as shown:

Your quadruped should now look similar to the following image:

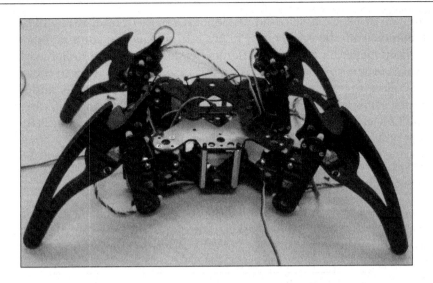

Now that you have the basic hardware assembled, you can turn your attention to the electronics.

Using a servo controller to control the servos

To make your quadruped walk, you first need to connect the servo motor controller to the servos. The servo controller you are going to use for this project is a simple servo motor controller using USB from Pololu: Pololu item number 1354, available at `https://www.pololu.com/`, which can control 18 servo motors. Here is an image of the unit:

Make sure you order the assembled version. This piece of hardware will turn the USB commands from the Raspberry Pi Zero into signals that control your servo motors. Pololu makes a number of different versions of this controller; each version can control a certain number of servos. In this case, you may want to choose the 18-servo version, so you can control all 12 servos with one controller and also add an additional servo to control the direction of a camera or sensor; you can also choose the 12-servo version. One advantage of the 18-servo controller is the ease of connecting power to the unit via screw-type connectors.

There are two connections that you'll need to make to the servo controller to get started: the first to the servo motors, the second to a battery.

First, connect the servos to the controller. In order to be consistent, let's connect your 12 servos to the connections marked 0 through 11 on the controller using the following configuration:

Servo connector	Servo
0	Right front lower leg
1	Right front middle leg
2	Right front upper leg
3	Right rear lower leg
4	Right rear middle leg
5	Right rear upper leg
6	Left front lower leg
7	Left front middle leg
8	Left front upper leg
9	Left rear lower leg
10	Left rear middle leg
11	Left rear upper leg

Here is an image of the back of the controller; this will tell us where to connect our servos:

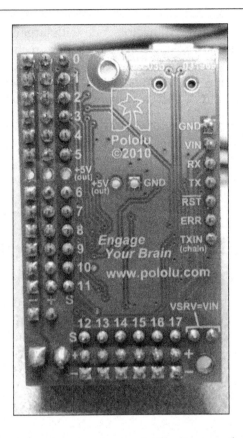

Now you need to connect the servo motor controller to your battery. For this project, you can use a 2S RC LiPo battery. The 2S means that the battery will have two cells, with an output voltage of 7.2 volts. It will supply the voltage and current needed by your servos, which can be in the order of 2 amps, as shown in the following image:

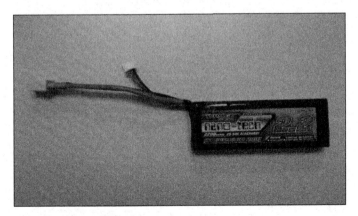

This battery will come with two connectors, one with larger gauge wires for normal usage and a smaller connector to connect to the battery recharger. You'll want to build connectors that can connect to the screw-type connectors of the servo controller. I purchased a few XT60 connector pairs and soldered some wires to the mating connector of the battery and then screwed these into the servo controller.

Your system is now functional. Now you'll connect the motor controller to your personal computer to check whether you can communicate with it. To do this, connect a mini USB cable to the servo controller and your personal computer. I'll detail the directions with a PC, but you can also do this step with a Mac or Linux. You can find the details at `https://www.pololu.com/docs/0J40`.

Communicating between the servo controller and a PC

Now that the hardware is connected, you can use some software provided by Pololu to control the servos. Let's do this using your personal computer. First, download the Pololu software from `www.pololu.com/docs/0J40/3.a` and install it based on the instructions on the website. Once it is installed, run the software and you should be able to see this screen:

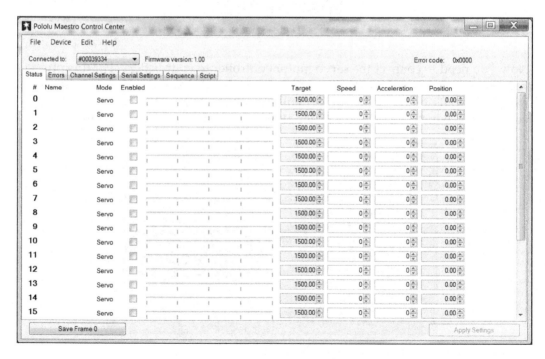

You will first need to change the configuration in **Serial Settings**, so select the **Serial Settings** tab, and you should see this:

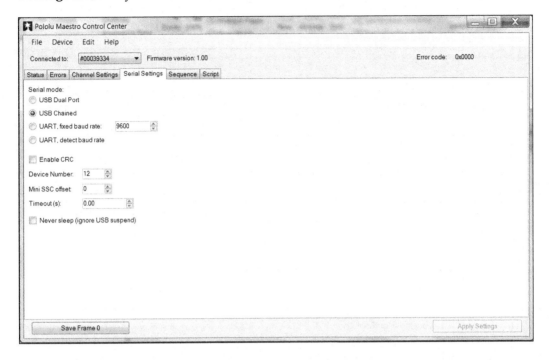

Make sure that **USB Chained** is selected; this will allow you to connect and control the motor controller over USB. Now go back to the main screen by selecting the **Status** tab; now you can actually turn on the 12 servos. The screen should look like this:

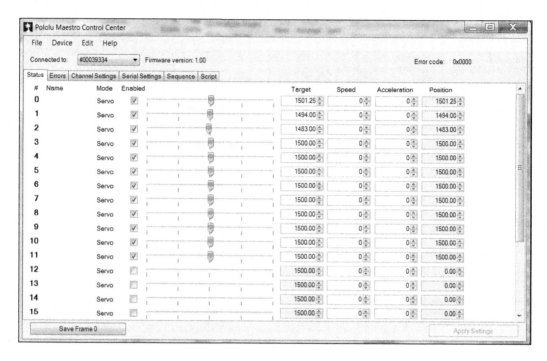

You can now use the sliders to actually control the servos. Make sure that servo 0 moves the right front lower servo, 1 the right front middle servo, 2 the right front upper servo, and so on. You can also use this to center the servos. Set all the servos so that the slider is in the middle. Now, unscrew the servo horn on each servo until the servos are centered at this location. At the zero location for all of your servos your quadruped should look like this:

Your quadruped is now ready to actually do something. Now, you'll need to send the servos the electronic signals they need to move your quadruped.

Connecting the servo controller to the Raspberry Pi Zero

You've checked the servo motor controller and the servos; you'll now connect the motor controller to the Raspberry Pi Zero and make sure that you can control the servos from it. Remove the USB cable from the PC and connect it to the Raspberry Pi Zero. The entire system will look similar to the following image:

The Raspberry Pi Zero is in the middle, the motor controller is to the right, and the powered hub to the left. The alligator clips below are connected to a power supply; eventually you'll want to connect these to a battery.

Let's now talk to the motor controller by downloading the Linux code from Pololu at `www.pololu.com/docs/0J40/3.b`:

1. Perhaps the best way is to log on to your Raspberry Pi Zero through PuTTY, then type `wget http://www.pololu.com/file/download/maestro-linux-100507.tar.gz?file_id=0J315`.

2. Then, move the file using `mv maestro-linux-100507.tar.gz\?file_id\=0J315 maestro-linux-100507.tar.gz`.

3. Unpack the file by typing `tar -xzfv maestro-linux-100507.tar.gz`.

4. This will create a directory called `maestro_linux`. Go to that directory by typing `cd maestro_linux` and then type `ls -l`; you should see something similar to this:

The document `README.txt` will give you explicit instructions on how to install the software. This is basically done in two steps:

1. First, install a set of supporting libraries by typing `sudo apt-get install libusb-1.0-0-dev mono-runtime libmono-winforms2.0-cil`.

2. Then, copy the configuration file by typing `sudo cp 99-pololu.rules /etc/udev/rules.d/`.

Unfortunately, you can't run Maestro Control Center on your Raspberry Pi Zero because your version of Windows doesn't support the graphics, but you can control your servos using the UscCmd command-line application to ensure that they are connected and working correctly.

First, type ./UscCmd --list and you should see the following:

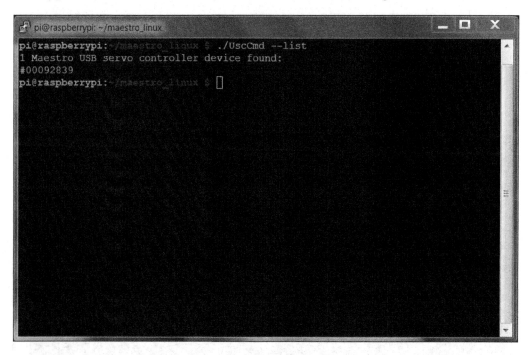

The unit sees our servo controller. If you just type ./UscCmd, you can see all the commands you can send to your controller:

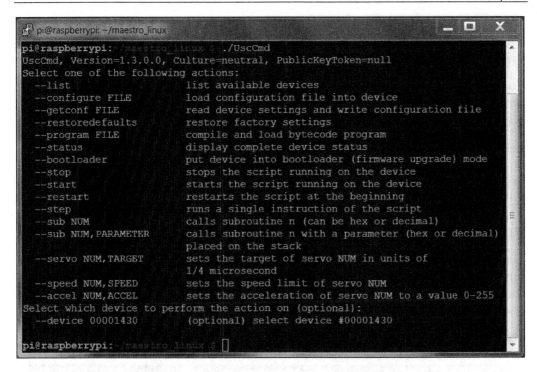

```
pi@raspberrypi: ~/maestro_linux
pi@raspberrypi:   /maestro linux $  ./UscCmd
UscCmd, Version=1.3.0.0, Culture=neutral, PublicKeyToken=null
Select one of the following actions:
  --list                    list available devices
  --configure FILE          load configuration file into device
  --getconf FILE            read device settings and write configuration file
  --restoredefaults         restore factory settings
  --program FILE            compile and load bytecode program
  --status                  display complete device status
  --bootloader              put device into bootloader (firmware upgrade) mode
  --stop                    stops the script running on the device
  --start                   starts the script running on the device
  --restart                 restarts the script at the beginning
  --step                    runs a single instruction of the script
  --sub NUM                 calls subroutine n (can be hex or decimal)
  --sub NUM,PARAMETER       calls subroutine n with a parameter (hex or decimal)
                            placed on the stack
  --servo NUM,TARGET        sets the target of servo NUM in units of
                            1/4 microsecond
  --speed NUM,SPEED         sets the speed limit of servo NUM
  --accel NUM,ACCEL         sets the acceleration of servo NUM to a value 0-255
Select which device to perform the action on (optional):
  --device 00001430         (optional) select device #00001430

pi@raspberrypi:   /maestro linux $ []
```

Note that you can send a servo a specific target angle, although the target is not in degrees of angle values so it makes it a bit difficult to know where you are sending your servo.

Try typing ./UscCmd --servo 0, 10. The servo will move to its full angle position.

Type ./UscCmd - servo 0, 0 and it will stop the servo from trying to move.

In the next section, you'll write some Python code that will translate your angles into commands that the servo controller will want to move it to specific angle locations.

If you didn't run the Windows version of Maestro Controller and set the **Serial Settings** to **USB Chained**, your motor controller may not respond. Rerun the Maestro Controller code and set the **Serial Settings** to **USB Chained**.

Creating a program in Linux to control your quadruped

You now know that you can talk to your servo motor controller and move your servos. In this section, you'll create a Python program that will let you talk to your servos to move them to specific angles.

Let's start with a simple program that will make your legged mobile robot's servos go to 90 degrees (which should be somewhere close to the middle of the 0 to 180 degrees you can set.) To access the serial port, you'll need to make sure that you have the Python serial library. If you don't, then type `sudo apt-get install python-serial`. After you have installed the serial library, you can run your program by typing `sudo python quad.py`.

This particular controller uses two bytes of information, so the code in the `setAngle` function will translate the input of the channel and angle into numbers that the controller can understand. For more specifics, see `http://www.pololu.com/docs/0J40`. Here is the code:

```
pi@raspberrypi: ~/maestro_linux

File Edit Options Buffers Tools Python Help
#!/usr/bin/python
import serial
import time

def setAngle(ser, channel, angle):
    minAngle = 0.0
    maxAngle = 180.0
    minTarget = 256.0
    maxTarget = 13120.0
    scaledValue = int((angle / ((maxAngle - minAngle) / (maxTarget - minTarget))) + minTarget)
    commandByte = chr(0x84)
    channelByte = chr(channel)
    lowTargetByte = chr(scaledValue & 0x7F)
    highTargetByte = chr((scaledValue >> 7) & 0x7F)
    command = commandByte + channelByte + lowTargetByte + highTargetByte
    ser.write(command)
    ser.flush()

ser = serial.Serial("/dev/ttyACM0", 9600)
# Home position
for i in range(0, 12):
    setAngle(ser, i, 90)
time.sleep(1)

-UU-:----F1  robot.py       All L1      (Python) --------------------------------
For information about GNU Emacs and the GNU system, type C-h C-a.
```

Here is an explanation of the code:

- `#! /usr/bin/python`: This first line allows you to execute this Python file from the command line.

- `import serial`: This line imports the `serial` library. You need the `serial` library to talk to your unit via USB.
- `def setAngle(ser, channel, angle):`: This function converts your desired setting for servo and angle into the serial command that the servo motor controller needs.
- `ser = serial.Serial("/dev/ttyACM0", 9600)`: This opens the serial port connection to your servo controller.
- `for i in range(0, 12):`: This `for` loop will access each servo.
- `setAngle(ser, i, 90)`: Now, you can set each servo to the middle (home) position. The default would be to set each servo to 90 degrees. If your legs aren't in their middle position, you can adjust them by adjusting the position of the servo horns on each servo.

Once you have the basic home position set, you can now ask your robot to do things. Let's start by making your quadruped wave. Here is the Python code:

```
pi@raspberrypi: ~/maestro_linux
File Edit Options Buffers Tools Python Help
#!/usr/bin/python
import serial
import time

def setAngle(ser, channel, angle):
    minAngle = 0.0
    maxAngle = 180.0
    minTarget = 256.0
    maxTarget = 13120.0
    scaledValue = int((angle / ((maxAngle - minAngle) / (maxTarget - minTarget)\
)) + minTarget)
    commandByte = chr(0x84)
    channelByte = chr(channel)
    lowTargetByte = chr(scaledValue & 0x7F)
    highTargetByte = chr((scaledValue >> 7) & 0x7F)
    command = commandByte + channelByte + lowTargetByte + highTargetByte
    ser.write(command)
    ser.flush()

ser = serial.Serial("/dev/ttyACM0", 9600)
# Home position
for i in range(0, 12):
    setAngle(ser, i, 90)
setAngle(ser, 1, 110)
time.sleep(1)
setAngle(ser, 0, 130)
time.sleep(1)
setAngle(ser, 0, 100)
time.sleep(1)
setAngle(ser, 0, 130)
time.sleep(1)
setAngle(ser, 0, 100)
time.sleep(1)
setAngle(ser, 0, 90)
time.sleep(1)
setAngle(ser, 1, 190)
time.sleep(1)
ser.close()

-UU-:----F1  robotWave.py   Top L1     (Python) --------------------------------
Wrote /home/pi/maestro_linux/robotWave.py
```

In this case, you are using the `setAngle` command to set your servos to manipulate your robot's front-right arm. The middle servo raises the arm and the lower survey then goes back and forth between angle 100 and 130 degrees.

One of the most basic actions you'll want your robot to take is to walk forward. Here is an example of how to manipulate the legs to make this happen:

```
pi@raspberrypi: ~/maestro_linux
File Edit Options Buffers Tools Python Help

ser = serial.Serial("/dev/ttyACM0", 9600)
# Home position
for i in range(0, 12):
    setAngle(ser, i, 90)

setAngle(ser, 4, 110)
time.sleep(1)
setAngle(ser, 5, 100)
time.sleep(1)
setAngle(ser, 4, 90)
time.sleep(1)

setAngle(ser, 7, 70)
time.sleep(1)
setAngle(ser, 8, 80)
time.sleep(1)
setAngle(ser, 7, 90)
time.sleep(1)

setAngle(ser, 1, 110)
time.sleep(1)
setAngle(ser, 2, 100)
time.sleep(1)
setAngle(ser, 1, 90)
time.sleep(1)

setAngle(ser, 10, 70)
time.sleep(1)
setAngle(ser, 11, 80)
time.sleep(1)
setAngle(ser, 10, 90)
time.sleep(1)

for i in range(0, 12):
    setAngle(ser, i, 90)

ser.close()

-UU-:----F1  robotWalk.py   47% L53   (Python) ----------------
Wrote /home/pi/maestro_linux/robotWalk.py
```

This program lifts and then moves each leg forward, one at a time, then moves all the legs to the home position, which moves the robot forward. Not the most elegant, but it does work. There are more sophisticated algorithms for walking with your quadruped; see `http://letsmakerobots.com/node/35354` and `https://www.youtube.com/watch?v=jWP3RnYa_tw`. Once you have the program working, you'll want to package all your hardware onto the mobile robot.

You can make your robot do many amazing things, such as walk forward, walk backward, dance, and turn around; any number of movements are possible. The best way to learn is to try new and different positions with the servos.

Summary

You now have a robot that can walk! You can also add other sensors, such as the ones you discovered for your wheeled robot, sensors that can watch for barriers, or others that know the direction you are moving in.

In the next chapter, you'll start on a new robot. You'll combine a Raspberry Pi Zero with a toy robot and construct a project with the ability to speak and respond to voice commands.

6
Adding Voice Recognition and Speech – A Voice Activated Robot

You've started with some pretty basic projects but you can take the concepts you have learned further by modifying robotic toys with the Raspberry Pi Zero. One class of toys that are excellent candidates for your projects are a set of robot toys by WowWee. You can purchase these toys from the company at `http://wowwee.com/` but you can also find used versions of these toys on eBay for a significantly lower price.

In this chapter, you'll learn the following:

- How to break into the toy and provide the control signals for your project
- How to send and receive voice commands to control the robot
- How to interpret commands and initiate actions

There are several toys that have excellent possibilities. One such toy is the **WowWee Roboraptor**. The following picture shows this robot:

Another option is the **WowWee Robosapien**. Here is a picture of this one:

We will use this robot for the project, as it has more functionality and is easier to modify.

Communication between the Raspberry Pi Zero and the robot

You're going to connect to the internal serial bus so that you, not the remote, can send commands. You'll add an Arduino to handle real-time communication between the Raspberry Pi Zero and the robot. Here are the steps:

1. Firstly, you need to disassemble the robot to get access to the main controller board. To do this, lay the robot face down so that you have access to the back. Remove the plate at the back by unscrewing the four screws that hold it in place. Now, at the top of the exposed board, you should see the main connector. The following image is a close-up photograph of the connector:

There are only two wires that you are interested in. The first is the black wire, which is the GND for the Robosapien system. The second is the white wire. This is the serial connection that controls the command for the Robosapien.

2. So, you're going to connect a wire to the black wire, but you need both ends of the black wire to stay connected to the system. To do this, strip off a bit of the insulation with a soldering iron and then solder another wire at this point. The following image illustrates this:

3. Now, snip the white wire and connect a wire to the end that is connected to the white header connector, as shown in this image:

You may want to add some heat-shrink tubing to cover your connections.

4. Finally, drill a hole in the back shell of the robot so that you can run both of these cables out of the unit, as shown in the following image:

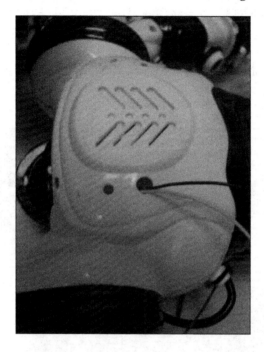

5. This picture also shows two more holes on either side of the shell, which you can use together with cable ties to attach the Raspberry Pi to the robot. Now you can put the shell back onto the robot.

6. Now, you need to connect these two wires to the Arduino. There are several versions of the Arduino that work but the most common one is the Arduino Uno. If you use a different Arduino with a different time, the delay constant in the Arduino code may need adjusting. The reason that you need to use an Arduino is that the bit patterns that are sent to the robot are sent at a fairly high rate and need to be created by a processor dedicated to this type of real-time communication. This allows the Raspberry Pi Zero to perform other processor-intensive activities, such as speech, while keeping the communication flowing at the correct rate.

For specifics on how to use the development environment of the Arduino family of processors, visit `https://www.arduino.cc`. For information on how to use the Raspberry Pi to create and upload programs to the Arduino, refer to `http://www.instructables.com/id/Arduino-On-Pi/` or `https://www.youtube.com/watch?v=wCxQrW96jTM`.

7. Connect the GND wire to one of the GND pins on the Arduino. Then, connect the other wire to pin 9 on the Arduino. These connections should look similar to the following picture:

8. The final step is to get the code to send the correct commands to the Arduino board. The code for this book is available in the PacktPub code download section or at `http://playground.arduino.cc/Main/RoboSapienIR`. This Arduino code takes an input from the **Serial Monitor**, in this case a USB connection from the Raspberry Pi Zero and turns it into the appropriate command for the WowWee robot. Once you have uploaded the code to the Arduino, either by using an external PC or a Raspberry Pi Zero, you can use the Arduino IDE's Serial Monitor capability to send individual letter commands and the robot should respond to these commands.

If you are unfamiliar with the Arduino IDE application, Arduino is well documented at https://www.arduino.cc/ which includes instructions on how to upload the code and use the Serial Monitor to communicate with the Arduino.

Now that the robot works, you can add the following Python program to send the commands:

```
pi@raspberrypi: ~/wowee
File Edit Options Buffers Tools Python Help
#!/usr/bin/python

import serial
import sys

ser = serial.Serial('/dev/ttyACM0', 9600, timeout = 1)
total = len(sys.argv)
cmdargs = str(sys.argv)

if total > 1:
    x = sys.argv[1]
    ser.write(x);
    s = ser.read(100);
#    print s

-UU-:----F1  argControl.py   All L1     (Python)----------------------------
For information about GNU Emacs and the GNU system, type C-h C-a.
```

To run this program, type `python argControl.py f` and the robot will respond to that command. To make this program executable without the Python command, type `chmod +x argControl.py` and you will be able to run the program by typing `./argControl.py f`. You'll need this later when you want to run this program from your voice control program.

Giving your robot voice commands

Now that your robot knows how to respond to the commands from the Python program, you can add the ability to your robot to respond to voice commands. You'll also make your robot speak, which will make the robot more interactive.

To add these capabilities to your robot, you need to add some new hardware. This project requires a USB microphone and speaker adapter. You need the following three pieces of hardware:

- A USB device to be able to plug in a microphone and speaker; one that works well is Sabrent USB External Stereo Sound Adapter for Windows and Mac, as shown here:

- A microphone that can plug into the USB device; any such device might work, like the one shown here:

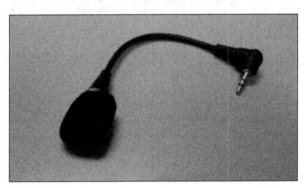

- A powered speaker that can plug into the USB device; any device that can plug into your USB adapter would work, such as something similar to what is shown here:

Fortunately, these devices are inexpensive and widely available. Make sure that the speaker is powered because your board will generally not be able to drive a passive speaker with enough power for your applications. The speaker can use either internal battery power or can get its power from a USB connection.

Now, we move on to getting the Raspberry Pi Zero to access these devices. You can follow these instructions in either of the two following ways:

- If you are still connected to the display, keyboard, and mouse, log in to the system and use the GUI by opening a terminal window
- If you are only connected through LAN, you can do all this by using an SSH terminal window; as soon as your board indicates that it has power, open up an SSH terminal window using PuTTY or any similar terminal emulator

Plug the devices into a USB port. Once the terminal window comes up, type `cat /proc/asound/cards`. You will get the following response:

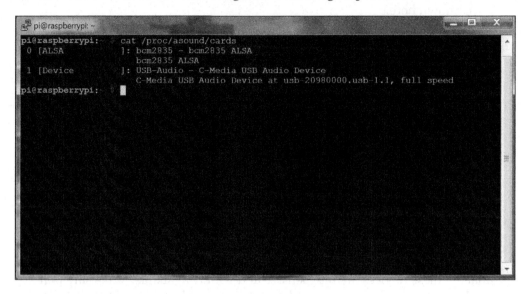

There are two possible audio devices that you can use. The first is the internal Raspberry Pi audio, which is connected to the audio port, and the second is the USB audio plugin. You could use the USB audio plugin to record the sound and the Raspberry Pi for the audio output to play the sound, though it is easier to just use the USB audio plugin to create and record sound.

Firstly, you need to play some music to test whether the USB sound device is working or not. You need to configure your system to search for your USB audio plugin and use it as the default plugin to play and record sound. To do this, you need to add a couple of libraries to your system. The first libraries are the **Advanced Linux Sound Architecture (ALSA)** libraries. These will enable the sound on the Raspberry Pi if you perform the following steps:

1. Install two libraries that are associated with ALSA by typing `sudo apt-get install alsa-base alsa-utils`.

2. Then, install those files that help to provide the sound library by typing `sudo apt-get install libasound2-dev`.

You'll use an application named **alsamixer** to control the volume of the input and output of your USB sound card. To do this, perform the following steps:

1. Type `alsamixer` at the command prompt. You will see a screen similar to the following screenshot:

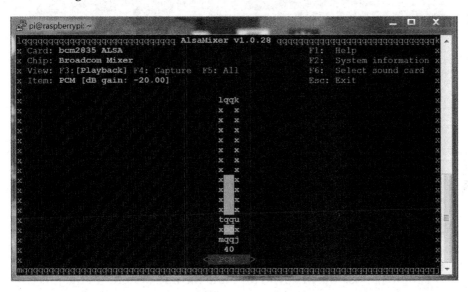

2. Press *F6* and select your USB sound device by using the arrow keys. This is demonstrated in the following screenshot:

3. `C-Media USB Audio Device` is my USB audio device. You should now be able to see a screen that looks similar to the following screenshot:

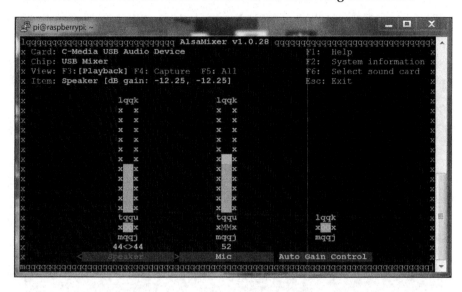

4. You can use the arrow keys to set the volume for both the speakers and the microphone. Use the *M* key to un-mute the microphone. In the preceding screenshot, `MM` is mute and `oo` is un-mute.

5. Let's make sure that our system knows about our USB sound device. At the command prompt, type `aplay -l`. You should now be able to see the following screenshot:

```
pi@raspberrypi: ~
pi@raspberrypi:   $ aplay -l
**** List of PLAYBACK Hardware Devices ****
card 0: ALSA [bcm2835 ALSA], device 0: bcm2835 ALSA [bcm2835 ALSA]
  Subdevices: 8/8
  Subdevice #0: subdevice #0
  Subdevice #1: subdevice #1
  Subdevice #2: subdevice #2
  Subdevice #3: subdevice #3
  Subdevice #4: subdevice #4
  Subdevice #5: subdevice #5
  Subdevice #6: subdevice #6
  Subdevice #7: subdevice #7
card 0: ALSA [bcm2835 ALSA], device 1: bcm2835 ALSA [bcm2835 IEC958/HDMI]
  Subdevices: 1/1
  Subdevice #0: subdevice #0
card 1: Device [C-Media USB Audio Device], device 0: USB Audio [USB Audio]
  Subdevices: 1/1
  Subdevice #0: subdevice #0
pi@raspberrypi:   $
```

If this does not work, try `sudo aplay -1`. You need to add a file to your home directory called `.asoundrc`. This will be read by your system and used to set your default configuration. To do this, perform the following steps:

1. Open the file named `.asoundrc` using the editor of your choice.
2. Type `pcm.!default sysdefault:Set`. `Set` is the variable that appears right after `card 1:` in the output of the `aplay -1` command.
3. Save the file. The file should appear as follows:

This will tell the system to use your USB device as the default. Reboot your system.

Now, you can play some music. To do this, you need a sound file and a device to play it. You can copy a simple `.wav` file to your Raspberry Pi Zero. If you are using a Linux machine as your host, you can also use the `scp` command from the command line to transfer the file. You can download music onto the Raspberry Pi Zero by using a web browser if you have a keyboard, mouse, and display connected. You use the application named **aplay** to play sound. Type `aplay Dance.wav` to see whether you can play music using the aplay music player. You will see the result (and hopefully hear it), as shown in the following screenshot:

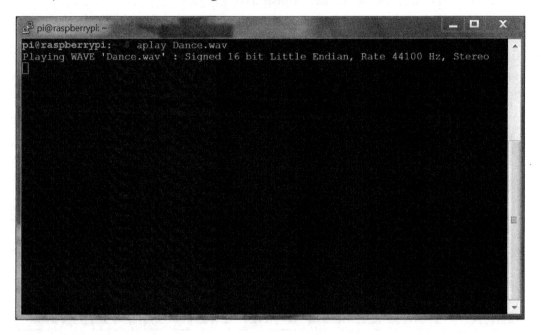

If you don't hear any music, check the volume level on alsamixer and the speaker power cable; aplay can be a bit finicky about the types of file it accepts, so you may be required to try different `.wav` files until aplay accepts one. One more thing to try, if the system doesn't seem to know about the program, is to type `sudo aplay Dance.wav`.

Now that you can play sound, you can also record sound. To do this, you have to use the **arecord** program. At the prompt, type `arecord -d 5 -r 48000 test.wav`. This records the sound at a sample rate of 48000 Hz per 5 seconds. Once you have typed the command, either speak into the microphone or make some other recognizable sound. You will see the following output in the terminal:

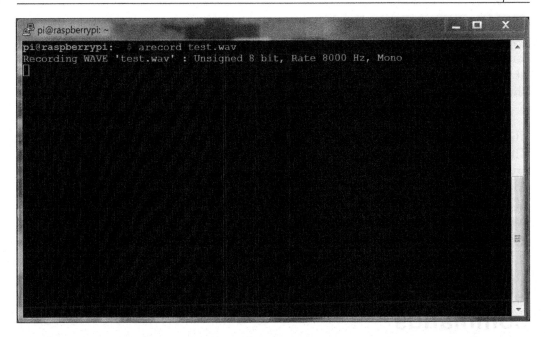

Once you have recorded some audio, stop the recording by pressing *Ctrl + C*. Once you have created the file, play it with aplay. Type `aplay test.wav` and you should be able to hear the recording. If you can't hear your recording, check alsamixer to make sure that your speakers and microphone are both un-muted.

Now you can play music or other sound files using your Raspberry Pi. You can change the volume of your speaker and record your voice or other sounds on the system. You're now ready for the next step.

Using eSpeak to allow your robot to respond with an audible voice

Sound is an important tool in our robotic toolkit but you will want to do more than just play music. Let's make our robot speak. You're going to start by enabling **eSpeak**, an open source application that provides us with a computerized voice. It is a voice generation application. To get this free functionality, download the `eSpeak` library by typing `sudo apt-get install espeak` at the prompt. The download may take a while but the prompt will reappear when it is complete. Now, let's see if the Raspberry Pi Zero has a voice. Type the `espeak hello` command. The speaker should emit "hello" in a computer-generated voice. If it does not, check the speakers and the volume level.

Now that we have a computer-generated voice, you may want to customize it. eSpeak offers a complete set of customization features, including a large number of languages, voices, and other options. To access these, you can type in the options at the command-line prompt. For example, type in `espeak -v +f3 hello` and you should be able to hear a female voice. You can even add a Scottish accent by typing `espeak -v en-sc +f3 hello`.

There are a lot of choices with respect to the voices that you can use with eSpeak. This depends on your own preferences but you might like a female voice with an English accent. Feel free to play around and choose your favorite voice. Then, edit the default file to set it to this voice. This default file is in the home directory of eSpeak. However, don't expect to get the kinds of voice that you hear from computers in the movies; those are actors and not computers. However, one day, we will hopefully reach a stage when computers will sound a lot more like real people.

Using pocketsphinx to accept your voice commands

Now that your robot can talk, you'll also want it to obey voice commands. This section shows you how to add speech recognition to your robotic projects. This isn't nearly as simple as the speaking part but, thankfully, you have some significant help from the open source development community. You are going to download a set of capabilities named **pocketsphinx**, which will allow our project to listen to our commands.

The first step is downloading the pocketsphinx software. Unfortunately, this is not quite as user-friendly as the eSpeak process, so follow these steps carefully. There are two ways to do this. If you have a keyboard, mouse, and display connected or want to connect through vncserver, you can do this graphically by performing the following steps:

1. Go to the Sphinx website hosted by **Carnegie Mellon University (CMU)** at `http://cmusphinx.sourceforge.net`. This is an open source project that provides you with speech recognition software. With our smaller embedded system, we will use the pocketsphinx version of this code.

2. You will need to download two pieces of software—**sphinxbase** and pocketsphinx. Select the **DOWNLOAD** option at the top of the page and then find the latest version of both of these packages. Download the `.tar.gz` versions of the packages and move them to the `/home/pi` directory of your Raspberry Pi.

Another way to do this is to use **wget** directly from the command prompt of the Raspberry Pi. If you want to do it in this way, perform the following steps:

1. To use wget on your host machine, find the link to the file that you wish to download. In this case, go to the Sphinx website hosted by CMU at `http://cmusphinx.sourceforge.net`. This is an open source project that provides you with the speech recognition software. With your smaller embedded system, you will use the pocketsphinx version of this code.

2. You will need to download two pieces of software, namely sphinxbase and pocketsphinx. Select the **DOWNLOAD** option at the top of the page and then find the latest version of both these packages. Right-click on the `sphinxbase-0.8.tar.gz` file (as long as 0.8 is the latest version) and select **Copy link location**. Now open a PuTTY window in your Raspberry Pi and, after logging in, type `wget` and paste the link that you just copied. This will download the `.tar.gz` version of sphinxbase. Now, follow the same procedure for the latest version of pocketsphinx.

Before you build these, you need another library. This library is called **Bison**. This is a general purpose, open source parser that is used by pocketsphinx. To get this package, type `sudo apt-get install bison`.

Once everything is downloaded and the libraries are installed, you can untar and build pocketsphinx. To unpack and build the sphinxbase module, type `sudo tar -xzvf sphinxbase-0.y.tar.gz`, where `y` is the version number, which in this example is `8`. This should unpack all the files from the archive into a directory named `sphinxbase-0.8`. Now, type `cd sphinxbase-0.8`. The listing of the files should look something like the following screenshot:

To build the application, start by issuing the `sudo ./configure --enable-fixed` command. This command checks whether or not everything is okay with the system and then configures a build.

Now you are ready to build the sphinxbase codebase. This is a two-step process, which is as follows:

1. Type `sudo make` and the system will build all the executable files.
2. Type `sudo make install` to install all the executables onto the system.

Now, you need to make the second part of the system — the pocketsphinx code. Go to the home directory and decompress and unarchive the code by typing `tar -xzvf pocketsphinx-0.8.tar.gz`. Now, the files will be unarchived and you can build the code. Installing these files is a three-step process, as follows:

1. Type `cd pocketsphinx-0.8` to go to the pocketsphinx directory and then type `sudo ./configure` to check whether or not you are ready to build the files.

2. Type `sudo make` and wait for everything to build.

3. Type `sudo make install`.

Other additions to our library installations will be useful later if you are going to use the pocketsphinx capability with Python as the coding language. You can install **Python-Dev** using `sudo apt-get install python-dev`. Similarly, you can get **Cython** using `sudo apt-get install cython`. You can also choose to install `pkg-config`, a utility that sometimes helps in dealing with complex compiles. Install it by using `sudo apt-get install pkg-config`.

Once the installation is complete, you need to let the system know where your files are. To do this, use your favorite editor and change the `/etc/ld.so.conf` file by adding a line to the file so that it looks as follows:

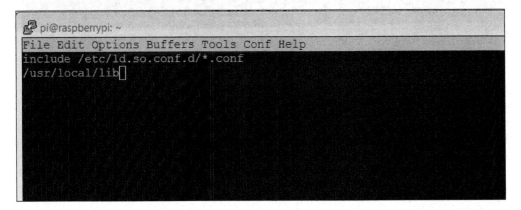

Type `sudo /sbin/ldconfig` and the system will be aware of your pocketsphinx libraries. Now that everything is installed, you can try out the speech recognition. Reboot the system and type `cd /home/pi/pocketsphinx-0.8/src/programs` to go to a directory to try a demo program. Then, type `./pocketsphinx_continuous`. For some reason, I had to type `sudo ./pocketsphinx_continuous`, allow it to fail, and then type `./pocketsphinx_continuous` to make it work. This program takes input from the microphone and turns it into speech. After running the command, you'll get a lot of irrelevant information and then you will see the following screenshot:

```
pi@raspberrypi: ~/pocketsphinx-0.8/src/programs
INFO: ngram_model_dmp.c(288):    436879 = LM.bigrams(+trailer) read
INFO: ngram_model_dmp.c(314):    418286 = LM.trigrams read
INFO: ngram_model_dmp.c(339):     37293 = LM.prob2 entries read
INFO: ngram_model_dmp.c(359):     14370 = LM.bo_wt2 entries read
INFO: ngram_model_dmp.c(379):     36094 = LM.prob3 entries read
INFO: ngram_model_dmp.c(407):       854 = LM.tseg_base entries read
INFO: ngram_model_dmp.c(463):      5001 = ascii word strings read
INFO: ngram_search_fwdtree.c(99): 788 unique initial diphones
INFO: ngram_search_fwdtree.c(147): 0 root, 0 non-root channels, 60 single-phone
words
INFO: ngram_search_fwdtree.c(186): Creating search tree
INFO: ngram_search_fwdtree.c(191): before: 0 root, 0 non-root channels, 60 singl
e-phone words
INFO: ngram_search_fwdtree.c(326): after: max nonroot chan increased to 13428
INFO: ngram_search_fwdtree.c(338): after: 457 root, 13300 non-root channels, 26
single-phone words
INFO: ngram_search_fwdflat.c(156): fwdflat: min_ef_width = 4, max_sf_win = 25
INFO: continuous.c(371): /home/pi/pocketsphinx-0.8/src/programs/.libs/lt-pockets
phinx_continuous COMPILED ON: Dec  6 2015, AT: 12:27:01

Warning: Could not find Mic element
Warning: Could not find Capture element
READY....
```

The `INFO` and `Warning` statements come from the C or C++ code and are there for debugging purposes. Initially, they will warn you that they cannot find your `Mic` and `Capture` elements but, when your Raspberry Pi finds them, it will print out `READY.....` If you have set things up as described previously, you are ready to give your Raspberry Pi a command. Say "hello" into the microphone. When it senses that you have stopped speaking, it will process your speech and, after giving lots of irrelevant information, it will eventually show the commands, as shown in the following screenshot:

```
pi@raspberrypi: ~/pocketsphinx-0.8/src/programs                    _  □  X
INFO: ngram_search_fwdtree.c(1557):      5275 words for which last channels evalu
ated (79/fr)
INFO: ngram_search_fwdtree.c(1560):      29399 candidate words for entering last p
hone (445/fr)
INFO: ngram_search_fwdtree.c(1562): fwdtree 1.92 CPU 2.909 xRT
INFO: ngram_search_fwdtree.c(1565): fwdtree 3.37 wall 5.100 xRT
INFO: ngram_search_fwdflat.c(302): Utterance vocabulary contains 134 words
INFO: ngram_search_fwdflat.c(937):      1773 words recognized (27/fr)
INFO: ngram_search_fwdflat.c(939):     91470 senones evaluated (1386/fr)
INFO: ngram_search_fwdflat.c(941):    154528 channels searched (2341/fr)
INFO: ngram_search_fwdflat.c(943):      8014 words searched (121/fr)
INFO: ngram_search_fwdflat.c(945):      6337 word transitions (96/fr)
INFO: ngram_search_fwdflat.c(948): fwdflat 0.78 CPU 1.182 xRT
INFO: ngram_search_fwdflat.c(951): fwdflat 0.81 wall 1.228 xRT
INFO: ngram_search.c(1266): lattice start node <s>.0 end node </s>.55
INFO: ngram_search.c(1294): Eliminated 0 nodes before end node
INFO: ngram_search.c(1399): Lattice has 196 nodes, 1498 links
INFO: ps_lattice.c(1365): Normalizer P(O) = alpha(</s>:55:64) = -467488
INFO: ps_lattice.c(1403): Joint P(O,S) = -479230 P(S|O) = -11742
INFO: ngram_search.c(888): bestpath 0.11 CPU 0.169 xRT
INFO: ngram_search.c(891): bestpath 0.13 wall 0.196 xRT
000000000: hello
READY....
```

Notice the `000000000: hello` command. It recognized your speech! You can try out other words and phrases too. The system is very sensitive so it may pick up background noise. You will also see that it is not very accurate. We'll deal with this in a moment. To stop the program, press *Ctrl + C*.

There are two ways to make your voice recognition more accurate. One is to train the system to understand your voice more accurately. This is rather complex but if you want to know more, go to the CMU pocketsphinx, website which was mentioned earlier in the chapter.

The second way to improve accuracy is to limit the number of words that your system uses to determine what you are saying. The default has literally thousands of word possibilities, so pocketsphinx may choose the wrong word if the two words are similar in sound. To avoid this, you can make your own dictionary to restrict the words that pocketsphinx has to choose from. To create your own dictionary, follow the instructions at `http://cmusphinx.sourceforge.net/wiki/tutorialdict`.

Your system can now understand your voice commands! In the next section of this chapter, you'll learn how to use this input to create a response.

Interpreting commands and initiating actions

Now that the system can both hear and speak, you'll want to provide the robot with the ability to respond to your speech and execute commands based on the speech input. Next, you're going to configure the system to respond to simple commands.

In order to respond, we're going to edit the continuous.c code in the /home/pi/src/programs directory. We could create our own C file but this file is already set up in the **make** system and is an excellent starting point. You can save a copy of the current file as continuous.c.old so that you can always go back to the starting program if required. Then, you need to edit the continuous.c file. It is very long and a bit complicated. However, you are looking for a specific section in the code, which is shown in the following screenshot. Look for the /* Exit if the first word spoken was GOODBYE */ comment line:

In this section of the code, the word has already been decoded and is held in the `hyp` variable. You can add the code here in order to make your system do things based on the value associated with the word that we decoded. Firstly, let's try to add the ability to respond to hello and goodbye commands to see whether or not we can get the program to respond to these commands. You need to make changes to the code in the following manner:

1. Find the `/* Exit if the first word spoken was GOODBYE */` comment

2. In the statement `if (strcmp(word, "goodbye") == 0)`, change word to `hyp` and `goodbye`

3. Insert brackets around the `break;` statement and add the `system("espeak" \"good bye\"");` statement just before the `break;` statement

4. Add the other `else if` statement to the clause by typing `else if (strcmp(hyp, "hello") == 0)`. Add brackets after the `else if` statement and, inside the brackets, type `system("espeak \"hello\"");`

The file should now look as follows:

```
pi@raspberrypi: ~/pocketsphinx-0.8/src/programs
File Edit Options Buffers Tools C Help
        /* Finish decoding, obtain and print result */
        ps_end_utt(ps);
        hyp = ps_get_hyp(ps, NULL, &uttid);
        printf("%s: %s\n", uttid, hyp);
        fflush(stdout);

        /* Exit if the first word spoken was GOODBYE */
        if (hyp) {
            sscanf(hyp, "%s", word);
            if (strcmp(word, "goodbye") == 0)
                break;
            else if (strcmp(word, "hello") == 0)
                {
                    system("espeak \"hello\"");
                }
        }

        /* Resume A/D recording for next utterance */
        if (ad_start_rec(ad) < 0)
            E_FATAL("Failed to start recording\n");
    }
-UU-:----F1  continuous.c   80% L334   (C/1 Abbrev) --------------
Wrote /home/pi/pocketsphinx-0.8/src/programs/continuous.c
```

Now you need to rebuild your code. As the make system already knows how to build the pocketsphinx_continuous program, it will rebuild the application if you make a change to the continuous.c file at any point. Simply type sudo make and the file will compile and create a new version of pocketsphinx_continuous. To run your new version, type ./pocketsphinx_continuous. Make sure that you type ./ at the start. Again, I had to type sudo ./pocketsphinx_continuous, allow it to fail, and then type ./pocketsphinx_continuous to make it work.

If everything was set up correctly, saying "hello" should result in a response of "hello" from your Raspberry Pi. Saying "goodbye" should elicit a response of "goodbye" and also shut down the program. Note that the system command can be used to run any program that runs from a command line. Now you can use this program to start and run other programs based on the commands. In this case, you need to change the code shown to call your Python code to issue the commands to the robot, as shown in the following screenshot:

```c
if (hyp) {
    sscanf(hyp, "%s", word);
    if (strcmp(word, "goodbye") == 0)
        break;
    else if (strcmp(word, "hello") == 0)
    {
        system("espeak \"hello\"");
    }
    else if (strcmp(word, "roar") == 0)
    {
        system("espeak \"roaring\"");
        system("sudo /home/pi/wowee/argControl.py A");
    }
    else if (strcmp(word, "hi five") == 0)
    {
        system("espeak \"hi five\"");
        system("sudo /home/pi/wowee/argControl.py u");
    }
}
```

In this case, you hook up only two of the very many commands that your robot can respond to; you can add the rest of the commands to your continuous.c file by using the same technique. Now, you can give your robot voice commands and it will obey them! Using the directions from the earlier section of this chapter, you can also control your robot remotely using single character commands and add a webcam. You have your very own robotic servant!

Summary

In this chapter, you've learned about the basics of hacking a toy robot using a Raspberry Pi. Feel free to experiment; you can see how easily you can play all sorts of games with your new toys. In the next chapter, you'll learn how to build a remote control vehicle that can go into a room and display what it sees back to a central location.

7
Adding Raspberry Pi Zero to an RC Vehicle

You've now built robots that can roll, walk, and respond to voice commands. In this chapter, you'll modify an RC car to add Raspberry Pi Zero to control the vehicle. Additionally, you'll add a webcam so that you can see what your car is seeing remotely.

In this chapter, you'll learn the following topics:

- How to modify an Xmods RC car using Raspberry Pi Zero
- How to set break into the control circuitry of the car and use the Raspberry Pi to control it
- How to use wireless communication to add remote control to the car
- How to add a webcam so you can control your car via **First Person View (FPV)**

Configuring and controlling an RC car with Raspberry Pi Zero

In this project, you'll be working on a simple RC car, similar to the one shown here:

This particular car is an Xmods car, originally sold by Radio Shack. However, the best place to get them now is eBay. The advantage of this particular set is that the inputs to the drive train and steering are very easy to access.

The following image shows the car with its center control mechanism exposed:

There are two connections that you will want direct access to. The first is the drive motor, and the second is the steering mechanism. For this particular model of RC car, the drive mechanism is in the rear. What you are normally looking for is two wires that will directly drive the DC motor of the car. In this system, there is a connector in the rear of the car; it looks similar to the following image:

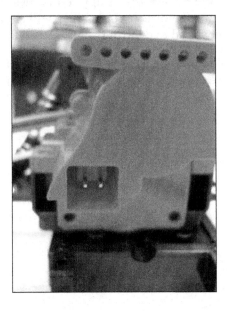

In the main control section of the car, you can see that there is a connector that plugs into these two wires, in order to control the speed of the car, as shown here:

Remove this plug and these wires; you'll use Raspberry Pi Zero and a motor controller to provide the voltage to the drive system of the car. The motor will run faster or slower based on the voltage that is applied to these wires and the polarity of the voltage will determine the direction. Raspberry Pi Zero will need to provide a positive or negative 6-volt signal to control the speed and direction of the car.

You'll also need to replace the control signals that go to the front of the car for the steering. This is a bit more difficult. The following is the connector that goes to the front of the car:

The five-pin connector that comes from the control module is shown in the following image:

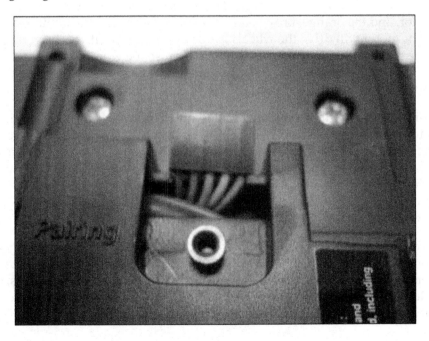

The trick is to determine how the wires control the steering. One way to determine this is by opening up the unit. This is how it looks from inside:

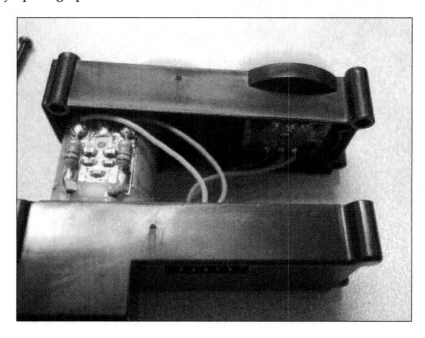

As you can see in the preceding image, the blue and yellow wires are attached to a DC motor, and the orange, brown, and red wires are attached to another control circuit. The motor will drive the wheels left or right, the polarity of the voltage will determine the direction, and its magnitude will cause the wheels to turn more or less sharply. The orange, brown, and red wires are interesting, as their purpose is a bit difficult to discover.

To do this, I used a voltmeter and an oscilloscope. The orange and brown wires are straightforward; they are 3.5 volts and GND, respectively. The red wire is a control wire; the signal is a **Pulse Width Modulation (PWM)** signal. It is a square wave at 330 Hz and 10 percent duty cycle, and it enables the control signal. Without the signal, the turning mechanism is not engaged. Now that you understand the signals that are used in the original system to control the car, you can replicate those with Raspberry Pi.

To control the steering, Raspberry Pi Zero needs to provide a 3.3-volt DC signal, a GND signal, a 330 Hz, 3.3-volt PWM signal, and the +/- 6-volt drive signal to the turning mechanism. To make these available, you can use the existing cables, solder some additional cable length and use some shrink-wrap tubing to create a new connector with the connector that is available in the car:

You'll also need access to the rear wheel compartment of your car to drive the two rear wheels. The following is how the access will look:

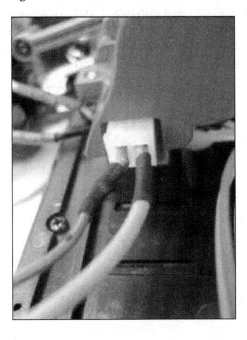

You'll also need to connect the battery power to Raspberry Pi Zero. Here is the modified connection to get the battery power from the car:

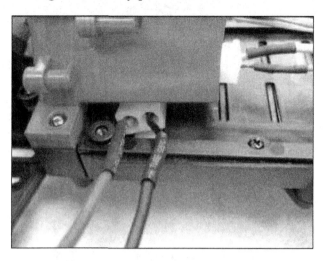

To control the car, you'll need to provide each of the control signals. The + or - 6-volt signals cannot be sourced directly by Raspberry Pi Zero. You'll need some sort of a motor controller to source the signal to control the rear wheel drive of the car and the turning mechanism of the car. The simplest way to provide these signals is to use a motor shield, an additional piece of hardware that is installed on top of Raspberry Pi Zero and can source the voltage and current to power both of these mechanisms. The RaspiRobot Board V2 you used in *Chapter 4, Building and Controlling a Simple Wheeled Robot*, can provide these signals, as shown in the following image:

Specifics on the board can be found at
http://www.monkmakes.com/?page_id=698.

The board will provide you with two key signals to your RC car, the drive signal and the turn signal. You'll need one more additional signal, the PWM signal that enables the steering control. The following are the steps to connect Raspberry Pi to the board:

1. First, connect the battery power connector to the power connector on the board, as shown in the following image:

2. Next, connect the rear drive signal to the motor 1 connectors on the board, as in the following image:

3. Connect the front drive connector to the motor 2 connectors on the board, as shown in the following image:

4. Connect the 3.3-volt and GND connectors to the **General Purpose Input/ Output (GPIO)** pins of Raspberry Pi. Here is a layout of these pins:

Pin 1 3.3V	□○	Pin 2 5V
Pin 3 GPIO2	○○	Pin 4 5V
Pin 5 GPIO3	○○	Pin 6 GND
Pin 7 GPIO4	○○	Pin 8 GPIO14
Pin 9 GND	○○	Pin 10 GPIO15
Pin 11 GPIO17	○○	Pin 12 GPIO18
Pin 13 GPIO27	○○	Pin 14 GND
Pin 15 GPIO22	○○	Pin 16 GPIO23
Pin 17 3.3V	○○	Pin 18 GPIO24
Pin 19 GPIO10	○○	Pin 20 GND
Pin 21 GPIO9	○○	Pin 22 GPIO25
Pin 23 GPIO11	○○	Pin 24 GPIO8
Pin 25 GND	○○	Pin 26 GPIO7
Pin 27 ID_SD	○○	Pin 28 ID_SC
Pin 29 GPIO5	○○	Pin 30 GND
Pin 31 GPIO6	○○	Pin 32 GPIO12
Pin 33 GPIO13	○○	Pin 34 GND
Pin 35 GPIO19	○○	Pin 36 GPIO16
Pin 37 GPIO26	○○	Pin 38 GPIO20
Pin 39 GND	○○	Pin 40 GPIO21

5. You'll use **Pin1 3.3V** for the 3.3-volt signal and **Pin 9 GND** for the ground signal. You'll connect one of the GPIO pins so that you can create the 320 Hz, 10 percent duty cycle signal to enable the steering. Connect GPIO pin 18, pin 12, as shown in the following image:

Now the hardware is connected.

Controlling the RC car in Python

The hardware is ready, now you can access all this functionality from Raspberry Pi Zero. First, install the library associated with the control board, found at `http://www.monkmakes.com/?page_id=698` and perform the following steps:

1. Run the command `wget https://github.com/simonmonk/raspirobotboard2/raw/master/python/dist/rrb2-1.1.tar.gz`. This will retrieve the library.

2. Then, run `tar -xzf rrb2-1.1.tar.gz`. This will unarchive the files.

3. Type `cd rrb2-1.1`. This will change the directory to the location of the files.

4. Type `sudo python setup.py install`. This will install the files.

Now you'll create some Python code that will allow you to access both the drive motor and the steering motor. The code will look similar to the following screenshot:

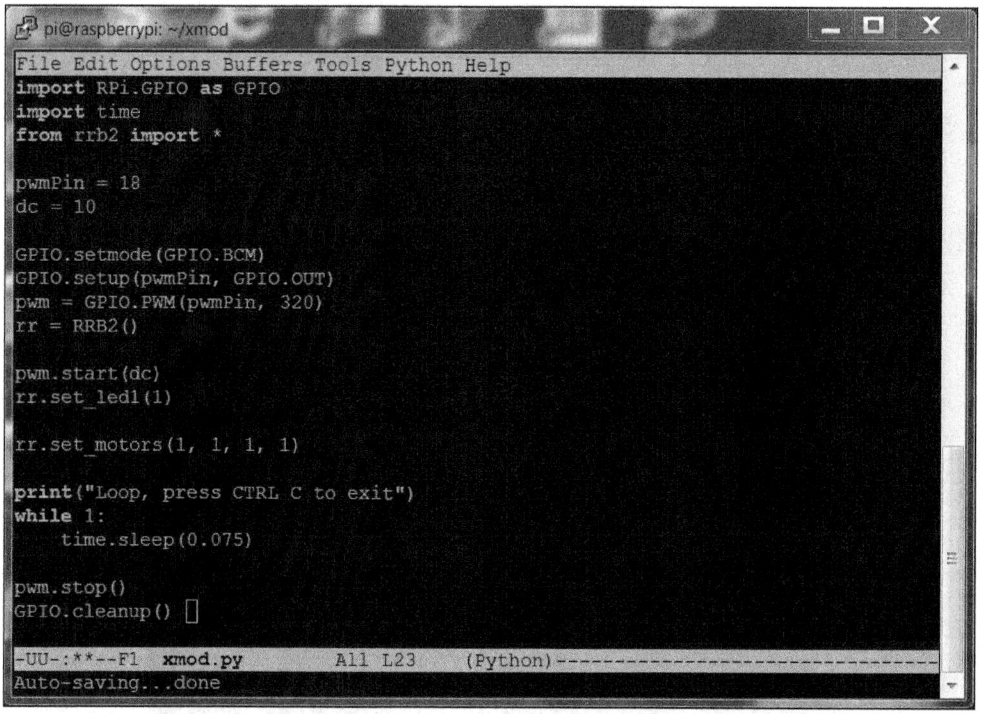

```
pi@raspberrypi: ~/xmod

File Edit Options Buffers Tools Python Help
import RPi.GPIO as GPIO
import time
from rrb2 import *

pwmPin = 18
dc = 10

GPIO.setmode(GPIO.BCM)
GPIO.setup(pwmPin, GPIO.OUT)
pwm = GPIO.PWM(pwmPin, 320)
rr = RRB2()

pwm.start(dc)
rr.set_led1(1)

rr.set_motors(1, 1, 1, 1)

print("Loop, press CTRL C to exit")
while 1:
    time.sleep(0.075)

pwm.stop()
GPIO.cleanup()

-UU-:**--F1   xmod.py        All L23      (Python)------------------------
Auto-saving...done
```

The specifics on the code are as follows:

- `import RPi.GPIO as GPIO`: This will import the `RPi.GPIO` library, allowing you to send out a PWM signal to the front steering mechanism.

- `import time`: This will import the `time` library, allowing you to use the `time.sleep(number_of_milliseconds)`, which causes a fixed delay.

- `from rrb2 import *`: This will import the `rrb2` library, allowing you to control the two DC motors. The `rrb2` is the library you just downloaded from GitHub.

- `pwmPin = 18`: This will set the PWM pin to GPIO pin 18, which is physical pin 12 on the Raspberry Pi.

- `dc = 10`: This will set the duty cycle to 10 percent on the PWM signal.

- `GPIO.setmode(GPIO.BCM)`: This will set the definition mode in the `RPi.GPIO` library to the BCM mode, allowing you to specify the GPIO numbers of the PWM signal.

- `GPIO.setup(pwmPin, GPIO.OUT)`: This will set the PWM pin to an output so that you can drive the control circuitry on the steering.

- `pwm = GPIO.PWM(pwmPin, 320)`: This will initialize the PWM signal on the proper pin and set the PWM signal to 320 Hz.

- `rr = RRB2()`: This will create an instance of the motor controller.

- `pwm.start(dc)`:This will start the PWM signal.

- `rr.set_led1(1)`: This will light LED 1 on the motor controller board.

- `rr.set_motors(1, 1, 1, 1)`:This will set both the motors to move so that the vehicle goes in the forward direction. This command will allow you to set the motors to forward or reverse and set it at a specific speed. The first number is the speed of motor 1 and goes from 0 to 1. The second number is the direction of motor 1, where 1 is forward and 0 is reverse. The third number is the speed of motor 2, which also goes from 0 to 1, and the fourth number is the reverse and forward setting of the second motor, either 1 or 0.

- `print("Loop, press CTRL C to exit")`: This will instruct the user how to stop the program.

- `while 1`: This will keep looping until *Ctrl + C* is pressed.

- `time.sleep(0.075)`: Causes the program to wait for 0.075 seconds.

- `pwm.stop()`: This will stop the PWM signal.

- `GPIO.cleanup()`: This will clean up the GPIO driver and prepare for shutdown.

Now you can run the program by typing `sudo python xmod.py`. When you run this, the LED 1 on the control board should turn on, the rear wheels should move in the forward direction, and the steering should turn. This confirms that you have connected everything correctly. To make this a bit more interesting, you can add more dynamic control of the motors by adding some control code. The following is the first part of the Python code:

```
pi@raspberrypi: ~/xmod
File Edit Options Buffers Tools Python Help
import RPi.GPIO as GPIO
import time
from rrb2 import *
import tty
import sys
import termios
def getch():
    fd = sys.stdin.fileno()
    old_settings = termios.tcgetattr(fd)
    tty.setraw(sys.stdin.fileno())
    ch = sys.stdin.read(1)
    termios.tcsetattr(fd, termios.TCSADRAIN, old_settings)
    return ch
pwmPin = 18
dc = 10
GPIO.setmode(GPIO.BCM)
GPIO.setup(pwmPin, GPIO.OUT)
pwm = GPIO.PWM(pwmPin, 320)
rr = RRB2()
pwm.start(dc)
rr.set_led1(1)
var = 'n'
speed1 = 0
speed2 = 0
direction1 = 1
direction2 = 1

while var != 'q':
    var = getch()
    if var == '1':
-UU-:**--F1   xmodControl.py    Top L1      (Python)---------------------
```

Before you start, you may want to copy your Python code into a new file; you can call it `xmodControl.py`. In this code, you'll have some additional `import` statements; these will allow you to sense key presses from the keyboard without hitting the enter key, this will make the real-time interface seem more real time. The `getch()` function senses the actual key press.

The rest of this code will look similar to the previous program. Now, the second part of this code is as follows:

```
pi@raspberrypi: ~/xmod                                    _  □  X
File Edit Options Buffers Tools Python Help
rr.set_led1(1)
var = 'n'
speed1 = 0
speed2 = 0
direction1 = 1
direction2 = 1

while var != 'q':
    var = getch()
    if var == 'l':
        speed1 = 0.5
        direction2 = 1
    if var == 'r':
        speed2 = 0.5
        direction2 = 0
    if var == 's':
        speed2 = 0.1
        direction = 1
    if var == 'f':
        speed1 = 1
        direction1 = 1
    if var == 'b':
        speed1 = 1
        direction1 = 0
    rr.set_motors(speed1, direction1, speed2, direction2)
    time.sleep(0.1)

pwm.stop()
GPIO.cleanup()

-UU-:**--F1   xmodControl.py    Bot L36    (Python)---------------------
```

The second part of the code is a `while` loop that takes the input and translates it into commands for your RC car, going forward and backward and turning right and left. This program is quite simple; you'll almost certainly want to add more commands that provide more ways to control the speed and direction.

Accessing the RC car remotely

You can now control your RC car, but you certainly want to do this without any connected cables. This section will show you how to add a wireless LAN device so that you can control your car remotely. In *Chapter 1*, *Getting Started with Raspberry Pi Zero*, you learned how to access Raspberry Pi Zero from a host computer. However, for this to work you need your Raspberry Pi Zero to be connected to a network, either with a LAN cable or a wireless network. What if you want to drive your car where there is no network, but still connect to it? You can do this by making your Raspberry Pi Zero a wireless access point.

Setting up Raspberry Pi Zero as a WLAN access point depends upon the USB WLAN adapter you choose; see `http://elinux.org/RPI-Wireless-Hotspot` for some of the devices supported and how to configure them. I chose the Edimax USB WLAN adapter, pictured here:

This device can be configured using the script found at `http://blog.sip2serve.com/post/48899893167/rtl8188-access-point-install-script`. Here are the steps:

1. Type `wget https://dl.dropboxusercontent.com/u/1663660/scripts/install-rtl8188cus.sh`. This gets the script content.

2. Type `sudo chown root:root install-rtl8188cus.sh`. This changes the owner so that you can install the script.

3. Type `sudo chmod 755 install-rtl8188cus.sh`. This changes the script's executable permission so you can execute it.

4. Finally, type `sudo ./install-rtl8188cus.sh` to run the script. This runs the script and configures the device. You will be asked for the name you want to use for the access point and the password.

This will pause and ask you if you want to continue to set up. Press *y*.

Now, you can connect your computer, tablet, or cell phone to the wireless access point. Using a terminal emulator program, like PuTTY, you can use the SSH protocol to access your device as described in *Chapter 1, Getting Started with Raspberry Pi Zero*. You can then execute your vncserver and run a vncviewer program on your remote device.

Connecting a webcam

Now you are ready to observe the output of a USB webcam connected to your car. This is quite straightforward; simply plug in a USB webcam and download a video viewer. One such video viewer that works well is guvcview. To install this, type sudo apt-get install guvcview.

With all these tools installed, you can now run vncview. When you are viewing the graphical screen of Raspberry Pi Zero type guvcivew -r 2 and you will be able to see the video from the webcam. You can control your RC car remotely by running the xcmodControl.py program that you wrote earlier. The screen will look similar to the following screenshot:

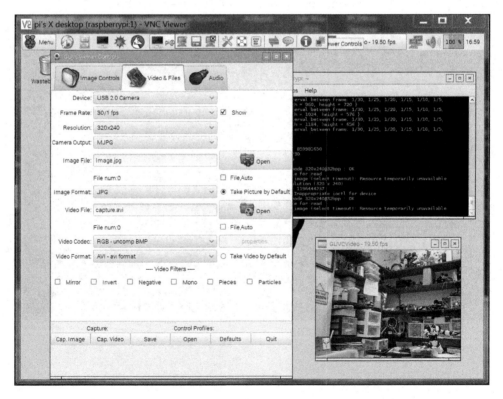

You will notice that as you adjust the resolution down, the update rate goes up; this is related to the size of the image. There are a lot of additions that you can make to your Raspberry Pi controlled car, such as adding the joystick control or more autonomy. However, let's move on to the next project.

Summary

Now you know how to work with Raspberry Pi to add its capability to an existing piece of hardware, in this case an RC car. In the next chapter, you'll learn how to use Raspberry Pi Zero to build a robot that can play rock, paper, or scissors.

8

Playing Rock, Paper, or Scissors with Raspberry Pi Zero

You've now built several projects with Raspberry Pi Zero. Now, you'll take some of these capabilities and add it to a new project, such as the ability to see and determine what is going on around you using a USB webcam and an open source library called **OpenCV**. In this project, you'll control a robotic hand to play the classic decision-making game; rock, paper, or scissors.

In this chapter, you will build a basic robotic hand and then use it to play rock, paper, or scissors. In this chapter, you will learn:

- How to use Raspberry Pi Zero to control servos that will control a robotic hand
- How to add a USB webcam to the project to "see" the world around you
- How to use OpenCV, an open source image processing library, to determine whether the human opponent is showing rock, paper, or scissors

A robotic hand

In this chapter, you'll build a human hand that has four fingers, a thumb, and a rotating wrist. There are actually several possible robotic hand configurations that you can purchase or build yourself. If you'd like to purchase an already 3D printed hand, my personal favorite is the hand that was designed by Christopher Chappelle and Easton LaChappelle, available already 3D printed at `http://www.shapeways.com/product/Z5CZ2RKLY/3d-printed-hand-right?li=search-results-1&optionId=42512474`. Here is an image of the hand:

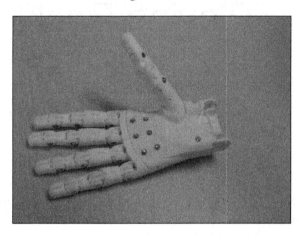

If you have access to a 3D printer, you can also download and print the hand yourself. Here is the link: `https://www.thingiverse.com/thing:288856`. Once you have assembled the hand, you'll need to add the servos to control the hand and the wrist. To control the hand, you'll pull on five separate fishing lines that come out of the hand. Here is an image of those fishing lines:

The hand is normally fully open. When you pull on the lines, each of the digits of the hand closes. When you release the lines, rubber bands on the back of each joint force the fingers and thumb back open. You'll use the servos to control the fingers and thumb. For this project, you'll only need three states: the fully-closed hand (rock), the fully-open hand with the sideways wrist (paper), and the thumb, ring finger and little finger closed with the index and pointer finger fully open (scissors).

Here is an image of how to connect the fishing lines to a servo:

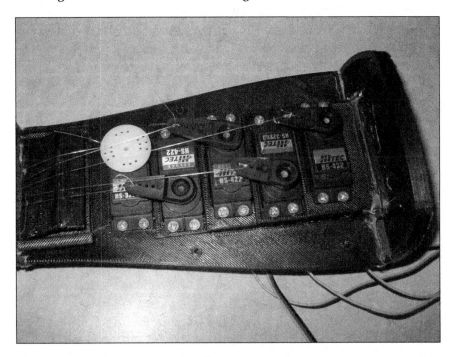

Connect each of the digits to a servo, and then connect the entire hand to a bracket; this will act as the wrist. You'll also connect this to a servo that can turn the wrist.

Moving the robotic hand

In order to move the servos, you'll use a servo controller similar to the one introduced in *Chapter 5, Building a Robot That Can Walk*, to control six servos that will control the fingers, thumb, and wrist. As in *Chapter 5, Building a Robot That Can Walk*, the servo controller you are going to use for this project is a simple servo motor controller using the USB from Pololu. However, since you only need to control five servos, you can order the six-servo controller version available at https://www.pololu.com. Here is an image of the unit:

Make sure you order the assembled version. This piece of hardware will turn the USB commands from the Raspberry Pi Zero into signals that control your servo motors. There are two connections that you'll need to make to the servo controller to get started: the first to the servo motors and the second to a power source.

First, connect the servos to the controller. In order to be consistent, let's connect your six servos to the connections marked 0 through 5 on the controller, using this configuration:

Servo connector	Servo
0	Thumb
1	Index finger
2	Middle finger
3	Ring finger
4	Little finger
5	Wrist

Here is an image of the back of the controller; this will tell us where to connect our servos:

Now, you need to connect the servo motor controller to a power source. For this project, you can use a battery but you can also use a dedicated power supply. Here is an image of a dedicated power supply, available at most on-line electronics outlets that can provide approximately 3 amps at 6 volts, which you'll need for the project:

The connections on the power supply are clearly marked; you'll connect the 6-volt power supply and GND connections to the connections marked BAT on the servo controller.

 Be very careful with this kind of power supply, never work on the wiring connected to the supply when the power supply is plugged in, and it is best to place the power supply in a protective enclosure after you have completed all the connections.

Your system is now functional. Now, you'll connect the motor controller to your personal computer to check to see if you can communicate with it as shown in *Chapter 5, Building a Robot That Can Walk*. To do this, connect a mini USB cable between the servo controller and your personal computer.

Now, you can use the sliders on the Pololu Maestro Control Center to actually control the servos. Make sure that servo 0 moves the thumb, 1 the index finger front middle servo, 2 the right front upper servo, and so on. You can also use this to calibrate the servos.

Set all of the servos so that the slider is on one side of the slider bar, as you will want this to be the open setting. The setting on the other side of the slider bar will pull the fishing line, and thus move the associated finger or thumb to the closed setting. Now, unscrew the servo horn on each servo until the servos are positioned so that the open hand is at one end of the servo's movement. When the servos move to the other end of the range, the hand should close.

Your hand is now ready to actually do something. Now, you'll need to send the servos the electronic signals they need to signal rock, paper, or scissors.

Connecting the servo controller to the Raspberry Pi Zero

You've checked the servo motor controller and the servos; you'll now connect the motor controller to the Raspberry Pi Zero and make sure you can control the servos from it. Remove the USB cable from the PC and connect it to the Raspberry Pi Zero.

Let's now focus on the motor controller by downloading the Linux code from Pololu at www.pololu.com/docs/0J40/3.b. Perhaps the best way is to log into your Raspberry Pi Zero through PuTTY, then type wget http://www.pololu. com/file/download/maestro-linux-100507.tar.gz?file_id=0J315. Then, move the file using mv maestro-linux-100507.tar.gz\?file_id\=0J315 maestro-linux-100507.tar.gz. Unpack the file by typing tar -xzfv maestro-linux-100507.tar.gz. This will create a directory called maestro_linux. Go to that directory by typing cd maestro_linux and then type ls -l; you should be able to see something similar to this:

```
pi@raspberrypi: ~/maestro_linux
pi@raspberrypi:~/maestro_linux $ ls -l
total 296
-rw-r--r-- 1 pi pi     55 May  7 2010 99-pololu.rules
-rw-r--r-- 1 pi pi  20480 May  7 2010 Bytecode.dll
-rw-r--r-- 1 pi pi  28672 May  7 2010 FirmwareUpgrade.dll
-rwxr-xr-x 1 pi pi 156160 May  7 2010 MaestroControlCenter
-rw-r--r-- 1 pi pi   4281 May  7 2010 README.txt
-rw-r--r-- 1 pi pi  11264 May  7 2010 Sequencer.dll
-rw-r--r-- 1 pi pi  12288 May  7 2010 UsbWrapper.dll
-rwxr-xr-x 1 pi pi  16384 May  7 2010 UscCmd
-rw-r--r-- 1 pi pi  37376 May  7 2010 Usc.dll
pi@raspberrypi:~/maestro_linux $
```

The document README.txt will give you explicit instructions
on how to install the software. This is basically done in two steps.
First, install a set of supporting libraries by typing sudo apt-get install
libusb-1.0-0-dev mono-runtime libmono-winforms2.0-cil, then copy the
configuration file by typing sudo cp 99-pololu.rules /etc/udev/rules.d/.

Unfortunately, you can't run Maestro Control Center on your Raspberry Pi Zero,
as your version of Windows doesn't support the graphics, but you can control your
servos using the UscCmd command-line application to ensure that they are connected
and working correctly. First, type ./UscCmd --list and you should be able to see
the following:

The unit sees your servo controller. If you just type ./UscCmd, you can see all the
commands you could send to your controller:

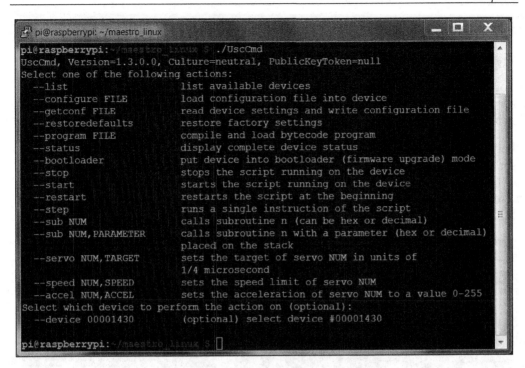

```
pi@raspberrypi: ~/maestro_linux
pi@raspberrypi:~/maestro_linux $ ./UscCmd
UscCmd, Version=1.3.0.0, Culture=neutral, PublicKeyToken=null
Select one of the following actions:
  --list                    list available devices
  --configure FILE          load configuration file into device
  --getconf FILE            read device settings and write configuration file
  --restoredefaults         restore factory settings
  --program FILE            compile and load bytecode program
  --status                  display complete device status
  --bootloader              put device into bootloader (firmware upgrade) mode
  --stop                    stops the script running on the device
  --start                   starts the script running on the device
  --restart                 restarts the script at the beginning
  --step                    runs a single instruction of the script
  --sub NUM                 calls subroutine n (can be hex or decimal)
  --sub NUM,PARAMETER       calls subroutine n with a parameter (hex or decimal)
                            placed on the stack
  --servo NUM,TARGET        sets the target of servo NUM in units of
                            1/4 microsecond
  --speed NUM,SPEED         sets the speed limit of servo NUM
  --accel NUM,ACCEL         sets the acceleration of servo NUM to a value 0-255
Select which device to perform the action on (optional):
  --device 00001430         (optional) select device #00001430

pi@raspberrypi:~/maestro_linux $ []
```

Note that you can send a servo to a specific target angle, although the target is not in degrees, so it makes it a bit difficult to know where you are sending your servo. Try typing ./UscCmd --servo 0, 10. The servo will move to its full angle position. Type ./UscCmd - servo 0, 0 and it will stop the servo from trying to move. In the next section, you'll write some Python code that will translate your angles in degrees to the commands that the servo controller will want to see in order to move it to specific angle locations.

If you didn't run the Windows version of Maestro Controller and set the **Serial Settings** to **USB Chained**, your motor controller may not respond. Rerun the Maestro Controller code and set the **Serial Settings** to **USB Chained**.

Creating a program on Raspberry Pi Zero so that you can control your hand

You now know that you can talk to your servo motor controller and move your servos. In this section, you'll create a Python program that will let you talk to your servos to move them to specific angles.

Let's start with a simple program that will position your hand so that the servos are set to one end of the range (which should open the hand) and then go the other end of the range (which should close your hand). This program starts with the code you wrote in *Chapter 5, Building a Robot That Can Walk*. Here is the basic code to control the servos:

```
pi@raspberrypi: ~/maestro_linux                                    _  □  X
File Edit Options Buffers Tools Python Help
#!/usr/bin/python
import serial
import time

def setAngle(ser, channel, angle):
    minAngle = 0.0
    maxAngle = 180.0
    minTarget = 256.0
    maxTarget = 13120.0
    scaledValue = int((angle / ((maxAngle - minAngle) / (maxTarget - minTarget))) + minTarget)
    commandByte = chr(0x84)
    channelByte = chr(channel)
    lowTargetByte = chr(scaledValue & 0x7F)
    highTargetByte = chr((scaledValue >> 7) & 0x7F)
    command = commandByte + channelByte + lowTargetByte + highTargetByte
    ser.write(command)
    ser.flush()

ser = serial.Serial("/dev/ttyACM0", 9600)
# Home position
for i in range(0, 12):
    setAngle(ser, i, 90)
time.sleep(1)

-UU-:----F1  robot.py       All L1     (Python) --------------------------------
For information about GNU Emacs and the GNU system, type C-h C-a.
```

Here is an explanation of the code:

- `#! /usr/bin/python`: This first line allows you to make this Python file execute from the command line.

- `import serial`: This line imports the serial library. You need the serial library to talk to your unit via USB.

- `def setAngle(ser, channel, angle):`: This function converts your desired setting of servo and angle into the serial command that the servo motor controller needs.

- `ser = serial.Serial("/dev/ttyACM0", 9600)`: This opens the serial port connection to your servo controller.

- `for i in range(0, 12):`: For each of the servos

- `setAngle(ser, i, 90)`: Now you can set each servo to the middle position. This should open your fingers half way. If your hand isn't in the middle position, you can adjust it by adjusting the position of the servo horns on each servo.

To access the serial port, you'll need to make sure that you have the Python serial library. If you don't, then type `sudo apt-get install python-serial`. After you have installed the serial library, you can run your program by typing `sudo python hand.py`.

Once you know the angle to set the servo at the middle angle position, the settings for the angle for each servo that opens or closes the hand will be roughly 20 degrees on either side. Finally, you can now ask your hand to close the servos for the thumb, ring finger, and little finger, which will be the scissors hand. You'll want a Python function for each of the three different positions. In this case, you can use your `setAngle` command to set your servos to manipulate your hand's six servos to either do paper (everything open), rock (everything closed), or scissors (two fingers extended, the rest closed).

Since each of these is a function, this code also has the ability to be included in a library so that they can be used in your system with the webcam.

Installing a USB camera on Raspberry Pi Zero

Having vision capability is essential to your rock, paper, or scissors robot. Fortunately, adding hardware and software for vision is both easy and inexpensive.

Connecting a USB camera is very easy. Just plug it into the USB slot. To make sure your device is connected, type `lsusb`. You should be able to see this:

```
pi@raspberrypi: ~
pi@raspberrypi ~ $ lsusb
Bus 001 Device 002: ID 0424:9514 Standard Microsystems Corp.
Bus 001 Device 001: ID 1d6b:0002 Linux Foundation 2.0 root hub
Bus 001 Device 003: ID 0424:ec00 Standard Microsystems Corp.
Bus 001 Device 004: ID 041e:4095 Creative Technology, Ltd
Bus 001 Device 005: ID 1ffb:008a
pi@raspberrypi ~ $
```

The following screen shows a creative webcam located at `Bus 001 Device 004: ID 041e:4095`. To make sure that the system sees this as a video device, type `ls /dev/v*` and you should see something similar to the following screenshot:

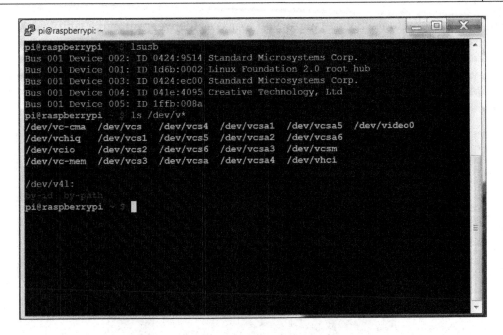

```
pi@raspberrypi  $ lsusb
Bus 001 Device 002: ID 0424:9514 Standard Microsystems Corp.
Bus 001 Device 001: ID 1d6b:0002 Linux Foundation 2.0 root hub
Bus 001 Device 003: ID 0424:ec00 Standard Microsystems Corp.
Bus 001 Device 004: ID 041e:4095 Creative Technology, Ltd
Bus 001 Device 005: ID 1ffb:008a
pi@raspberrypi  $ ls /dev/v*
/dev/vc-cma   /dev/vcs    /dev/vcs4   /dev/vcsa1   /dev/vcsa5   /dev/video0
/dev/vchiq    /dev/vcs1   /dev/vcs5   /dev/vcsa2   /dev/vcsa6
/dev/vcio     /dev/vcs2   /dev/vcs6   /dev/vcsa3   /dev/vcsm
/dev/vc-mem   /dev/vcs3   /dev/vcsa   /dev/vcsa4   /dev/vhci

/dev/v4l:
by-id  by-path
pi@raspberrypi  $
```

The `/dev/video0` is the webcam device. Now that your device is connected, let's actually see if you can capture the images and video.

 While many USB web cameras will work, in order to ensure this, you may want to purchase a webcam from a major webcam manufacturer like Logitech.

There are several tools that can allow you to access the webcam, but a simple program with video controls is called **guvcview**. To install this, type sudo apt-get install guvcview. Once the applications are installed, you'll want to run it. To do this, you'll need to be either connected directly to a display or connected to a remote computer using vncviewer. Open a terminal window on Raspberry Pi and run guvcview. You should see something similar to this:

Don't worry about the quality of the image, you'll be capturing and processing your images inside OpenCV, a vision framework.

Downloading and installing OpenCV – a fully featured vision library

Now that you have your camera connected, you can access some amazing capabilities that have been provided by the open source community. Open a terminal window and type the following commands:

- `sudo apt-get update`: You're going to download a number of new software packages, so it is good to make sure that everything is up to date.

- `sudo apt-get install libavformat-dev`: This library provides a way to code and decode audio and video streams.

- `sudo apt-get install libcv2.4 libcvaux2.4 libhighgui2.4`: This command shows the basic OpenCV libraries. Note the number in the command. This will almost certainly change as new versions of OpenCV become available. If 2.4 does not work, try either 3.0 or Google for the latest version of OpenCV.

- `sudo apt-get install python-opencv`: This is the Python development kit needed for OpenCV, as you are going to use Python.

- `sudo apt-get install opencv-doc`: This command will download the documentation for OpenCV just in case you need it.

- `sudo apt-get install libcv-dev`: This command downloads the header file and static libraries to compile OpenCV.

- `sudo apt-get install libcvaux-dev`: This command downloads more development tools for compiling OpenCV.

- `sudo apt-get install libhighgui-dev`: This is another package that provides header files and static libraries to compile OpenCV.

Now, type `cp -r /usr/share/doc/opencv-doc/examples /home/pi/`. This will copy all the examples to your home directory.

Now that OpenCV is installed, you can try one of the examples. Go to the `/home/pi/examples/python` directory. If you do an `ls`, you'll see a file named `camera.py`. This file has the most basic code for capturing and displaying a stream of picture images. But before you run the code, make a copy of it, using `cp camera.py myCamera.py`. Then edit the file to look similar to this:

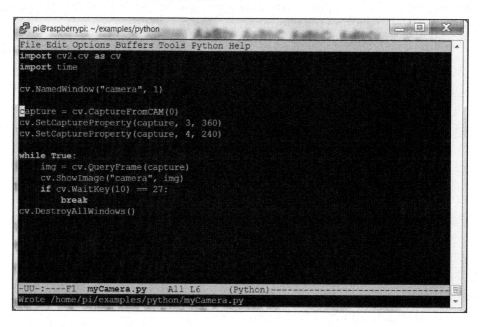

The two lines that you'll add are the two with the `cv.SetCaptureProperty`; they will set the resolution of the image to 360 by 240. To run this program, you'll need to either have a display and keyboard connected to Raspberry Pi or use vncviewer. When you run the code, you should see the window displayed as shown:

You may want to play with the resolution to find the optimum settings for your application. Big images are great—they give you a more detailed view of the world—but they also take up significantly more processing power. You'll play with this resolution more as you actually ask your system to do some real image processing. Be careful if you are going to use vncserver to understand your system performance, as this will significantly slow down the update rate. An image that is twice the size (width/height) will involve four times more processing. You can now use this capability to do a number of impressive tasks.

Gesture detection

OpenCV and your webcam can also track objects. This will be useful as you want your project to differentiate your hand from the background. OpenCV makes this amazingly simple by providing some high-level libraries that can help us with this task. To accomplish this, you'll edit a file to look something similar to what is shown in the following screenshot:

```
pi@raspberrypi: ~/examples/python
File Edit Options Buffers Tools Python Help
#!/usr/bin/python

import numpy as np
import cv2

cap = cv2.VideoCapture(0)
cap.set(3, 320)
cap.set(4, 240)
low_range = np.array([10, 120, 120])
high_range = np.array([70, 255, 255])

while (cap.isOpened()):
    ret, frame = cap.read()
    gray_image = cv2.cvtColor(frame, cv2.COLOR_BGR2GRAY)
    blur = cv2.GaussianBlur(gray_image,(5,5),0)
    ret, threshold_img= cv2.threshold(blur,80,255,cv2.THRESH_BINARY_INV+cv2.THRESH_OTSU)
    cv2.imshow('frame', threshold_img)
    if cv2.waitKey(10) == 27:
        break
cap.release()
cv2.destroyAllWindows()

-UU-:----F1  hand_gesture.py   All L1      (Python) ------------------------
For information about GNU Emacs and the GNU system, type C-h C-a.
```

This code makes it possible to isolate your hand. Once you have created this file and saved it, you can run the program. Now take your target (in this case your hand) and move it into the frame. You should see something similar to what is shown in the following screenshot:

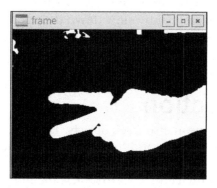

Note the white pixels in our threshold image showing where you hand is located. You can add more OpenCV code that gives the actual location and size of your hand. In the original image file of your hand, you can actually draw a rectangle around your hand as an indicator. Edit the file to look similar to the following screenshot:

```
import cv2
import numpy as np
import math

cap = cv2.VideoCapture(0)
cap.set(3, 320)
cap.set(4, 240)

def getHand():
    while(cap.isOpened()):
        ret, img = cap.read()
        cv2.rectangle(img, (200,200), (50,50), (0,255,0),0)
        crop_img = img[50:200, 50:200]
        grey = cv2.cvtColor(crop_img, cv2.COLOR_BGR2GRAY)
        value = (35, 35)
        blurred = cv2.GaussianBlur(grey, value, 0)
        _, thresh1 = cv2.threshold(blurred, 127, 255, cv2.THRESH_BINARY_INV+cv2.THRESH_OTSU)
        cv2.imshow('Thresholded', thresh1)
        contours, hierarchy = cv2.findContours(thresh1.copy(),cv2.RETR_TREE, cv2.CHAIN_APPROX_NONE)
        max_area = -1
        for i in range(len(contours)):
            cnt=contours[i]
            area = cv2.contourArea(cnt)
            if(area>max_area):
                max_area=area
                ci=i
        cnt=contours[ci]
        x,y,w,h = cv2.boundingRect(cnt)
        print x, y, w, h
        cv2.rectangle(crop_img, (x,y), (x+w,y+h), (0,0,255),0)
        cv2.imshow('Gesture', img)
        k = cv2.waitKey(10)
        if k == 27:
            break

getHand()
```

Now that the code is ready, you can run it. You should see something similar to what is shown in the following screenshot:

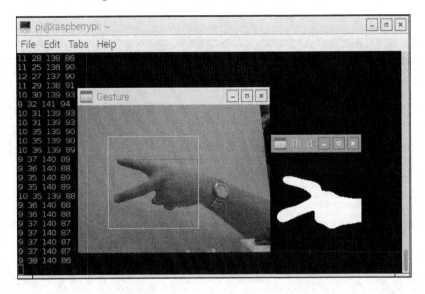

You can now track your hand. You can also see the *x*, *y*, length, and width relative measures of your hand for each of the scissors, rock, or paper. Here is the rock:

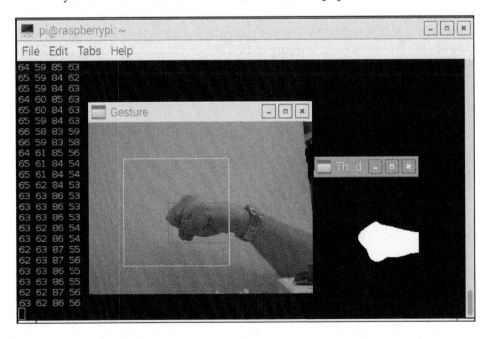

The following screen is the measure of your hand for paper:

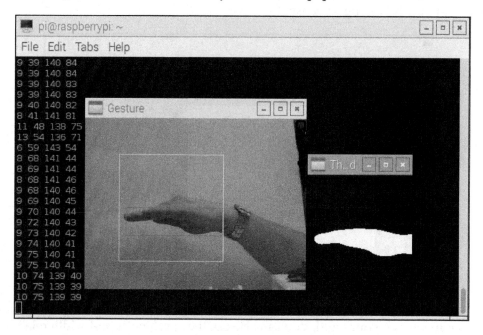

You can add some simple code to determine if your hand is making a rock, paper, or scissors using the ratios of x and y. In the preceding picture, you can see that the ratio of width to height is roughly 140/80 for paper. For a rock, the ratio is going to be roughly 85/55. For scissors, it is going to be 140/40. Here is the code for the library that determines a rock/paper/or scissors:

```
pi@raspberrypi: ~
File Edit Options Buffers Tools Python Help
import math

cap = cv2.VideoCapture(0)
cap.set(3, 320)
cap.set(4, 240)

def getHand():
    while(cap.isOpened()):
        ret, img = cap.read()
        cv2.rectangle(img, (200,200), (50,50), (0,255,0),0)
        crop_img = img[50:200, 50:200]
        grey = cv2.cvtColor(crop_img, cv2.COLOR_BGR2GRAY)
        value = (35, 35)
        blurred = cv2.GaussianBlur(grey, value, 0)
        _, thresh1 = cv2.threshold(blurred, 127, 255, cv2.THRESH_BINARY_INV+cv2.THRESH_OTSU)
        cv2.imshow('Thresholded', thresh1)
        contours, hierarchy = cv2.findContours(thresh1.copy(),cv2.RETR_TREE, cv2.CHAIN_APPROX_NONE)
        max_area = -1
        for i in range(len(contours)):
            cnt=contours[i]
            area = cv2.contourArea(cnt)
            if(area>max_area):
                max_area=area
                ci=i
        cnt=contours[ci]
        x,y,w,h = cv2.boundingRect(cnt)
        print x, y, w, h
        if w != 148 and h !=148: # not starting rectangle
            if w/h >= 3:
                return 3    # scissors
            elif w/h < 3 and w/h > 1:
                return 2
            else:
                return 3
        cv2.rectangle(crop_img, (x,y), (x+w,y+h), (0,0,255),0)
        cv2.imshow('Gesture', img)
        k = cv2.waitKey(10)
        if k == 27:
            break

print getHand()
-UU-:**--F1  rock_id.py     Bot L21    (Python) ---------------------------------
```

Now you know the state of the human opponent's hand. To complete the entire project, you'll need to add code to make a random selection for the computer hand's state, call the functions in the previous sections of this chapter to make the hand move to that state, and then compare the random selection of your robot hand and the user's hand to determine the winner. Playing rock, paper, or scissors has never been easier!

Summary

You now have a hand that can play rock, paper, or scissors! By now you should have quite a few different capabilities that you can add to almost any project. In the last chapter, you'll add Raspberry Pi Zero to a quad copter to build a project that can fly.

9
Adding Raspberry Pi Zero to a Quadcopter

You've had the opportunity to build lots of different types of robot, so now let's end with the one that can be truly amazing, a robot that can fly.

Before we start, there are a number of safety warnings to be considered. Of course, never fly near people or buildings. Also, be very careful about flying outside your viewing range. In many countries, there are restrictions on where and when you can fly a quadcopter. Some countries, including the United States, require you to register your quadcopter.

It is also important to note that this chapter is not designed to be a complete step-by-step guide to the construction of a quadcopter for flying. That would take many chapters. This chapter is designed to get you started if you consider building a quadcopter that can be controlled using the Raspberry Pi Zero. In this chapter, you'll learn about the following topics:

- Building the basic quadcopter platform
- Interfacing Raspberry Pi Zero with the flight controller
- Discussing long-range communications
- Using GPS for location
- Adding autonomous flight

Constructing the platform

Constructing the quadcopter hardware can be daunting; however, there are several excellent websites that can lead you through the process, from component selection to build details and programming and controlling your quadcopter with a radio. The `http://www.arducopter.co.uk/` website is a great place to start for those who are new to quadcopter flight. Go to `http://copter.ardupilot.com/`, which is another excellent website with lots of information.

For this project, you'll want to choose a project that uses the **Pixhawk** flight controller. There are other flight controllers that are significantly less expensive, but this particular flight controller provides easy access for Raspberry Pi Zero. Here are some possible websites that can guide you through the construction process: `http://learnrobotix.com/uavs/quadcopter-build/pixhawk/connecting-the-q-brain-esc.html`, `http://www.thedroneinfo.com/2015/06/06/build-a-quadcopter-with-pixhawk-flight-controller/`, and `http://www.flying-drone.co.uk/how-to-build-a-quadcopter-with-a-pixhawk-flight-controller-step-11/`.

At `http://copter.ardupilot.com/wiki/advanced-pixhawk-quadcopter-wiring-chart/`, you'll find an excellent wiring diagram of how to hook everything up. Let's go through the steps of constructing our own quadcopter.

First, you'll need a frame. You'll be building a quadcopter of size 450 mm, one of the least expensive frames, which is available from most online retailers, with fiberglass arms, as shown in the following image:

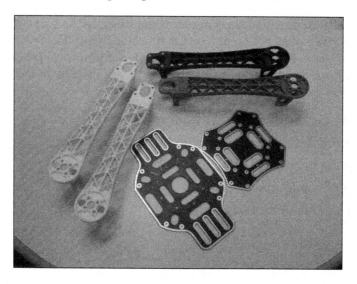

Now, perform the following steps to complete your quadcopter assembly:

1. The first step is to build the quadcopter as the instructions suggest.

2. The second step is to solder the four **Electronic Speed Controllers (ESCs)**, one to each motor, and the battery connection to the bottom plate. Here is an image of the bottom plate:

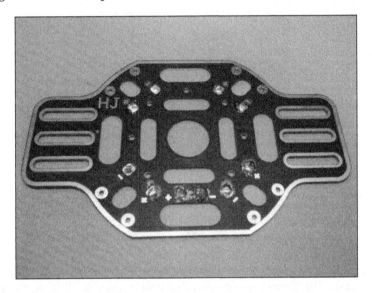

Note the + and – connections; each connection will be soldered to all the ESCs. The following is an image of the motor controller:

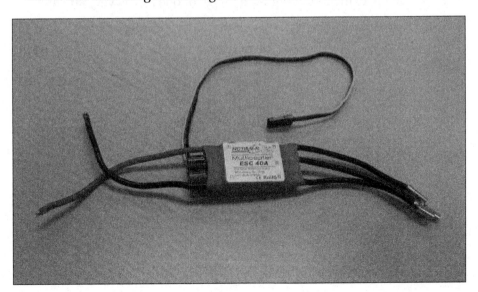

The red and black wire connectors are the connectors that are soldered to the bottom plate of the frame. The other three connectors will connect to the motor.

3. The third step is to install the motors on the frame. You'll need motors that are in the 1000 KV range, here is an image of such a motor:

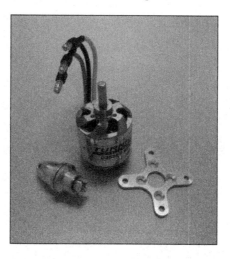

Again, follow the instructions that came with your frame to attach the motor. Then attach the three connections that come from the ESC to the motor.

4. One optional step is to add a landing gear set to the unit. There are many of these available; the following is an image of one that is very sturdy:

5. Now you'll install Pixhawk on the frame and connect its associated electronics. The details are shown and described at `http://copter.ardupilot.com/wiki/advanced-pixhawk-quadcopter-wiring-chart/`. This will connect the Pixhawk to the ESCs, the battery, an RC transmitter, a telemetry radio, and a switch that will prevent the quadcopter from flying until you are ready.

6. Eventually, you will install four propellers on the quadcopter; however, you will have to wait until you have calibrated the ESCs, motors, and RC transmitter to install them. You'll need four propellers, two that are designed to spin clockwise and another two that are designed to spin counter-clockwise. For this quadcopter, you'll want propellers that are 10x4.7 pitches. Here is an image of one such propeller:

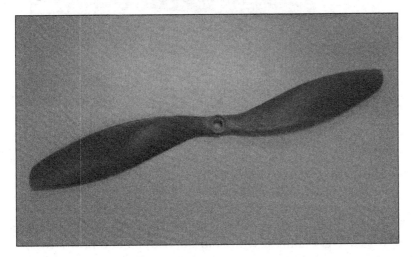

The following is an image of the entire quadcopter using the Pixhawk flight controller:

 Note the arrows and cords arranged on the quadcopter. This is not to make it look menacing but to protect it from running into something and fracturing the propellers. There are commercial guards available; however, this system also works and is less expensive.

You'll want to build your quadcopter and fly it with an RC transmitter/receiver pair; this will allow you to get familiar with your quadcopter and how it flies, and it will also allow you to tweak all the settings to stabilize it. Once your quadcopter is stable, you can perform some simple autonomous flights. Let's use the mission planning software, which runs on a remote computer.

Mission planning software

The mission planning software is available at http://planner.ardupilot. com/. There are actually two applications available that perform similar actions, but the **Mission Planner** is a good place to get familiar with how to talk with your quadcopter from a computer program.

To do this, you'll need to make sure that you have telemetry radios connected to the Pixhawk and the computer. This will prevent the need to directly connect to the Pixhawk with a long USB cable. When you begin the mission planning software, you will see the following screen:

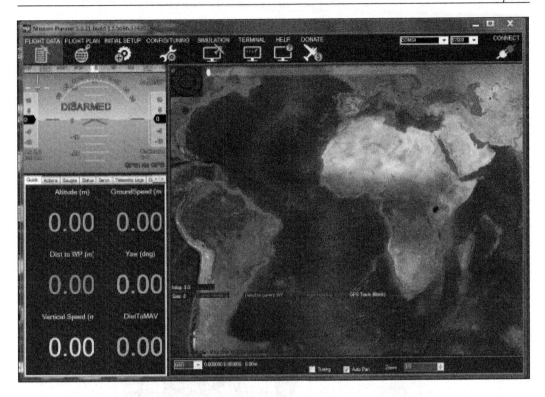

This is the basic screen. You'll then need to configure your radio's COM port and then press the **CONNECT** button in the corner on the upper right-hand side of the screen. As you move the quadcopter around, you will see the measurements change. If you are having problems connecting to the Pixhawk, there is lot of help available on the website.

Now that you have connected, you can actually see how your quadcopter is flying with this application. The software communicates with the Pixhawk controller via the **MAVLink**, a serial control link that comes from the software application, goes out over the telemetry radio, is received by the telemetry radio, and is then routed to the Pixhawk. The Pixhawk not only knows how to send information, but also receive information.

Once the software is connected, you'll want to calibrate the RC radio connection; this can be done through the software. You'll also want to calibrate the ESCs; refer to http://learnrobotix.com/uavs/quadcopter-build/pixhawk/calibrating-electronic-speed-controllers-with-pixhawk.html for specific directions.

Now, you are ready to connect the Raspberry Pi Zero. To do this, connect Raspberry Pi Zero to the second telemetry input on the Pixhawk, as shown in the following image:

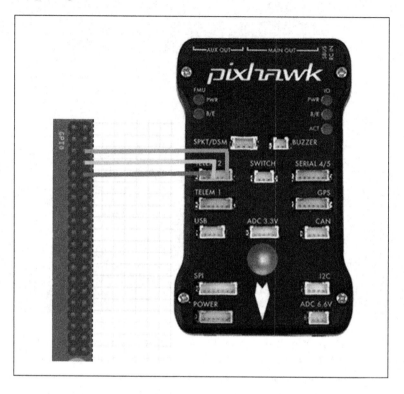

Now that this is connected, you can access the Pixhawk from Raspberry Pi Zero using the MAVLink. You'll need to add and configure the Raspberry Pi Zero to complete the connection. To do this, run `raspi-config` and choose the **8 Advanced Options, Configure advanced settings** option, as shown in the following screenshot:

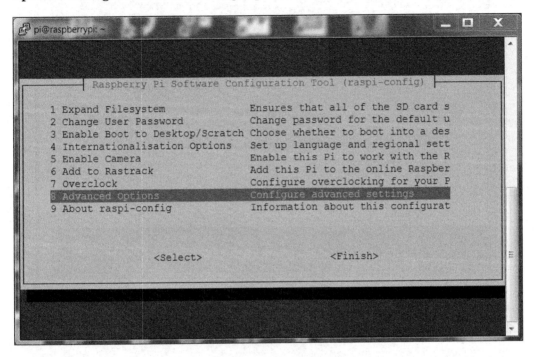

Now, you'll turn off sending the serial output on boot up by selecting the **A8 Serial, Enable/Disable shell and kernel m** option, as shown:

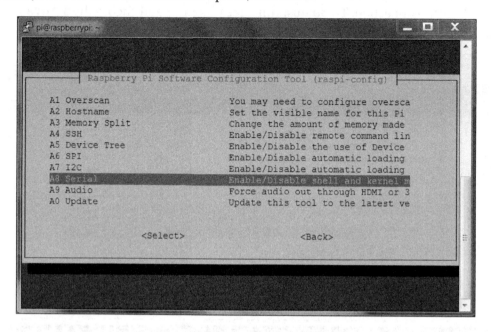

Then select the answer **<No>** to the following question:

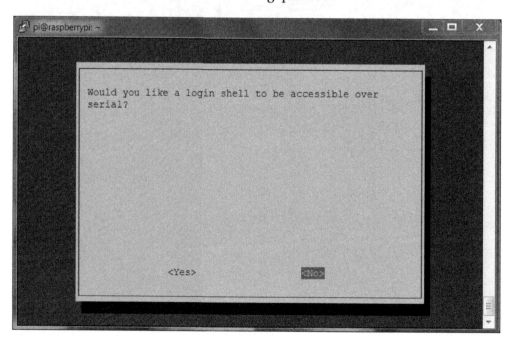

Now you are ready to install some additional software. To install this software, perform the following steps:

1. Type `sudo apt-get update`: This updates the local package lists so that your system can find the appropriate software.

2. Type `sudo apt-get install screen python-wxgtk2.8 python-matplotlib python-opencv`: This installs a graphical package, a plotting package, and a version of OpenCV.

3. Type `sudo apt-get install python-numpy`: This will install **NumPy**, a numerical library for Python, although you may already have it from the previous projects that you have done.

4. Type `sudo apt-get install python-dev`: This is a set of files that will allow you to develop in the Python environment.

5. Type `sudo apt-get install python-pip`: This is a tool that helps you to install Python packages.

6. Type `sudo pip install pymavlink`: This is the set of code that implements the MAVLink or the communication profile for the Pixhawk, in Python.

7. Type `sudo pip install mavproxy`: This last step installs the **Unmanned Aerial Vehicle (UAV)** ground station software package for MAVLink-based systems that are based on the Pixhawk.

Now that you have installed all the software, you can test the link. To do this, type `sudo -s`; this establishes you as the superuser. Then type `mavproxy.py --master=/dev/ttyAMA0 --baudrate 57600 --aircraft MyCopter` and you will see the following:

Now that the link is established, you can send commands to either `set` or `show` parameters. For example, type `param show ARMING_CHECK`; it should show you the value of the parameter, as shown in the following screenshot:

```
pi@raspberrypi: ~                                              _  □  X
Debian GNU/Linux comes with ABSOLUTELY NO WARRANTY, to the extent
permitted by applicable law.
Last login: Mon Sep 14 02:28:23 2015 from 116.98.25.36
pi@raspberrypi ~ $ sudo -s
root@raspberrypi:/home/pi# mavproxy.py --master=/dev/ttyAMA0 --baudrate 57600 --
aircraft MyCopter
Connect /dev/ttyAMA0 source_system=255
no script MyCopter/mavinit.scr
Log Directory: MyCopter/logs/2015-09-15/flight1
Telemetry log: MyCopter/logs/2015-09-15/flight1/flight.tlog
Waiting for heartbeat from /dev/ttyAMA0
MAV> 0 0 QAonline system 1
STABILIZE> Mode STABILIZE
fence breach
APM: ArduCopter V3.2.1 (36b405fb)
APM: PX4: ce602658 NuttX: 475b8c15
APM: Frame: QUAD
APM: PX4v2 00380029 31334706 38383835
Received 417 parameters
Saved 417 parameters to MyCopter/logs/2015-09-15/flight1/mav.parm

STABILIZE> param show ARMING_CHECK
STABILIZE> ARMING_CHECK    1.000000
```

Details for all available commands can be found at `http://dronecode.github.io/MAVProxy/html/uav_configuration/index.html`.

You can issue these commands directly, but you can also connect to the Pixhawk using an interface that is similar to the Mission Planner interface, which you have worked with earlier. To do this, you'll need to install the **DroneKit** code. Overall directions and documentation for DroneKit can be found at `http://python.dronekit.io/guide/getting_started.html#installing-dronekit`, but let's see an example here.

First, type `sudo pip install droneapi`. You can download some example scripts by typing `git clone http://github.com/dronekit/dronekit-python.git`. Now `cd` to the `dronekit-python/examples/vehicle_state` directory. You'll see the `vehicle_state.py` file that shows an excellent example of how to use the MAVLink to talk with the Pixhawk to find out information, as well as set values and issue commands.

To run an example program, start the MAVLink by typing two commands: `sudo -s`, and then `mavproxy.py --master=/dev/ttyAMA0 --baudrate 57600 --aircraft MyCopter`. Once inside, load the API by typing `module load droneapi.module.api` at the prompt. The system will then tell you whether the module is loaded. Now, run the Python script by typing `api start vehicle_state.py`.

The Python code will first read in a series of parameters and then, if the quadcopter is armed, it will also read some details about the state of the quadcopter. Details of each command can be found at `http://python.dronekit.io/guide/vehicle_state_and_parameters.html#vehicle-information`. The output will look something like the following screenshot:

```
pi@raspberrypi: ~/dronekit-python/examples/vehicle_state

STABILIZE> module load droneapi.module.api
STABILIZE> DroneAPI loaded
Loaded module droneapi.module.api

STABILIZE> api start vehicle_state.py
STABILIZE>
Get all vehicle attribute values:
 Location: Location:lat=0.0,lon=0.0,alt=1.38999998569,is_relative=False
 Attitude: Attitude:pitch=0.0657835155725,yaw=-3.04151630402,roll=-0.02454243041
57
 Velocity: [0.0, 0.0, 0.0]
 GPS: GPSInfo:fix=0,num_sat=0
 Groundspeed: 0.0
 Airspeed: 0.0
 Mount status: [None, None, None]
 Battery: Battery:voltage=0.0,current=None,level=None
 Rangefinder: Rangefinder: distance=None, voltage=None
 Rangefinder distance: None
 Rangefinder voltage: None
 Mode: STABILIZE
 Armed: False
Set Vehicle.mode=GUIDED (currently: STABILIZE)
 Waiting for mode change ...
Got MAVLink msg: COMMAND_ACK {command : 11, result : 0}
APM: PreArm: Need 3D Fix
GUIDED> Mode GUIDED
Set Vehicle.armed=True (currently: False)
 Waiting for arming...
Got MAVLink msg: COMMAND_ACK {command : 400, result : 3}
 Waiting for arming...
```

Now, you can look at other Python examples to see how to control your quadcopter via Python files from Raspberry Pi Zero.

You can also interface the **MAVProxy** system with the Mission Planner running on a remote computer. With a radio connected to the **TELEM 1** port of the Pixhawk and your Raspberry Pi Zero connected to the **TELEM 2** port of the Pixhawk, change the MAVProxy start-up command by adding `--out <ipaddress>:14550` with `ipaddress` being the address of the remote computer that is running the Mission Planner. On a Windows machine, the `ipconfig` command can be used to determine this IP address.

For example, your `mavproxy` command might look similar to this: `mavproxy.py --master=/dev/ttyAMA0 --baudrate 57600 --out ipaddress:14550 --aircraft MyCopter`. Once connected to MAVProxy, you can connect to the Mission Planner software using the UDP connection, as shown in the following screenshot:

Now, you can run your MAVProxy scripts and see the results on the Mission Planner software.

Summary

That's it. You now have a wide array of different robotics platforms that run with Raspberry Pi Zero as the central controller. These chapters have just introduced you to some of the most fundamental capabilities of your platforms; you can now explore each and expand their capabilities. The only limit is your imagination and time.

Index

CPSIA information can be obtained
at www.ICGtesting.com
Printed in the USA
LVOW04s1228020717
540116LV00004B/169/P